The Newmarch

Quest

A Thrilling Serendipitous Adventure

~ Finding a Millennium of Ancestral Treasures ~

Written & Illustrated
By Wendy L. Campbell

The Newmarch Quest
© Wendy Campbell

National Library of Australia Cataloguing-in-Publication entry

Author: Campbell, Wendy, author.

Title: The Newmarch Quest / Wendy Campbell.

ISBN: 9780992448400 (paperback)

Subjects: Newmarch family.

               England--Genealogy.

               Wales--Genealogy.

               France--Genealogy.

Dewey Number: 929.20942

Published with the assistance of www.loveofbooks.com.au

For my Dad

Colin Alfred Chapman

The Newmarch Quest

Preface

I'm so excited to be able to share this amazing story with you all. For those of you who share a common ancestor with me, I hope that my research will help to fill in some of the blanks for you. If you are one of the many who will simply enjoy the process and the thrill of the chase, I'm delighted that you can come along for the ride. Perhaps it may even inspire you to search out your own ancestral treasures!

When I began this 'quest', I had no idea that it would become such a juggernaut, slowly and unexpectedly 'drip feeding' me small details which, clue by clue led me into such a beautifully colourful, and historic panorama.

As the custodian of "The Newmarch Pedigree" for the last fifty years, I felt the heavy weight of responsibility upon my shoulders to try and make sense of its contents, and to be able to share that in some meaningful way, with my extended family, as a legacy for the generations to come, and to anyone else who will read and enjoy the journey.

I could never have imagined, however, the rewards that would follow.

I hope that Charles and George Newmarch, the authors of "The Newmarch Pedigree" would be pleased with with my efforts, I certainly am in awe of the pinpoint accuracy of their work, especially considering the resources available to them at the time of their writing.

Embarking on this adventure has not only enabled me to verify and confirm the assertions made by them almost 150 years ago, but above all, to experience every day the providential hand of God at work.

Enjoy,

Wendy L. Campbell

Gold Coast, Queensland,

Australia,

January, 2013.

Newmarch

The Newmarch Quest

Chapter 1

I want to tell you a true story, one that is filled with unexpected adventure and amazing serendipitous events, or if you're a believer as I am, God putting me in the right place at the perfect moment to meet the precise people or circumstance.

The story really begins almost 50 years ago, when as a 12-year-old girl, I was fascinated by a dusty faded green volume, held by my paternal grandmother, Harriet Gwenyth Newmarch, (or Big Nanny to my brother and me), and entitled,

"The Newmarch Pedigree,
Verified by
Public Records, Authentic Manuscripts, and General and Local Histories.
Printed for Private Circulation only."

It was fragile even then, having been written in 1868 by Geo. Fred. Newmarch and Chas. H. Newmarch, the pale green cardboard cover was now spineless and bore the remnant brown stains of previous sticky tape repairs.

The forty or so pages were thin and yellowing, even the pressure of the printing process had indented some of the letters through the pages as if expressing the importance of the document.

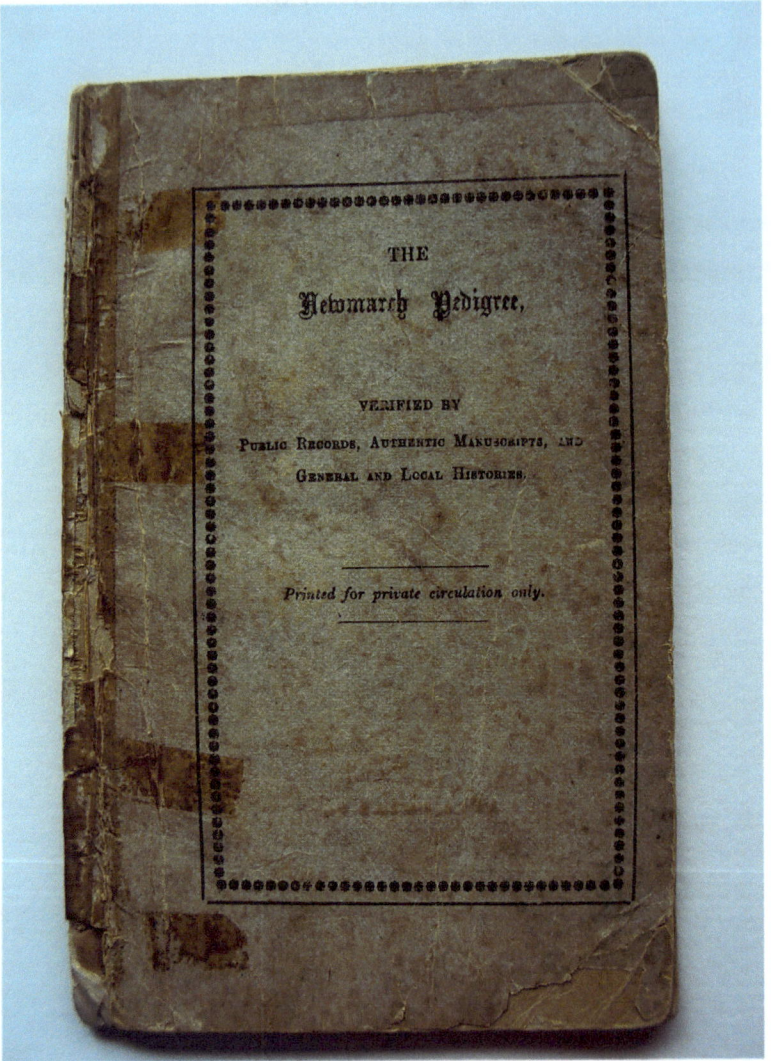

The Newmarch Pedigree – My Treasure Map!

As a 12 year old, I was amused by small things, such as the spelling of "antient", as well as the 'old English' used in the book, which contributed to me only being interested in the 'juicy' bits.

For me then, the thing that made the book so important and tantalizing, was the opening paragraph of Chapter 1, which read:

"A. D. 1066-1216.

BERNARD DE NOVO MERCATO, NEOFMARCHE, OR NEWMARCH, accompanied William the Conqueror on his invading England, A.D. 1066, some of the Welsh Pedigrees speaking of him as William's half brother."

Wow, how amazing! I needed to take this to school to show Miss Lyon! And so the precious volume was relinquished to my care, and came with me to school carefully wrapped in brown paper.

I'm ashamed to say that it has remained with me to this day, as I never gave it back to Big Nanny, and despite numerous inquiries over the years from concerned aunties and cousins as to its whereabouts and its welfare, it is still with me even escaping the total destruction of our home by fire, because it was in a chest in the shed and not in the house!

And so, almost half a century later, I felt that the onus was squarely on my shoulders to explore the book in depth and to find out what it really held in its pages besides the family's links with William the Conqueror.

As one who loves to travel, especially with a purpose, I thought that it would be wonderful to geographically follow

𝕮𝖍𝖊 𝕹𝖊𝖜𝖒𝖆𝖗𝖈𝖍 𝕻𝖊𝖉𝖎𝖌𝖗𝖊𝖊, which covers around 800 years of family history through France, Wales and England.

This was a great idea, and a wonderful reason to go travelling. How then was I going to go about it? I began by trawling through a copy of the family tree, noting and listing every place name mentioned, which I charted, showing the page number in the family tree, any significant event related to that place, and the map reference which was gleaned from super sized Great Britain and Europe road atlases.

I was amazed and thrilled that most of these place names, which were written about 143 years ago, and which in many cases referred to people or incidents which occurred almost 1,000 years ago, could still be found in the Great Britain atlas.

I marked the locations with an orange felt marker pen, the advantage of this was that I could see the 'big picture', with my orange dots scattered across the length and breadth of England and Wales, and across to Normandy in France. This strategy enabled me to plan the trip, which is not in any way my usual modus operandi, usually preferring to enjoy the surprises, which come along when no accommodation is booked, route planned or itinerary scheduled! For the purposes of this trip, as I wanted to visit as many places as possible, which were mentioned in the "book", a more defined schedule was required in the 3 weeks consigned to this Quest.

I split the time into, 2 weeks in England and Wales, and a week in France and deliberated as to the best pick up and drop off points for the rental cars.

As to accommodation, my first thought was to take my small two-man tent and camp, but fortuitously for me, whilst scanning the travel section of the local library for camping directories, I chanced upon "Lodging in Britain's Monasteries", by Eileen Barish. The idea of staying in such exotic old buildings containing rich tapestries of history, whilst tracing the footsteps of generations of my family through many centuries, was very appropriate and incredibly exciting!

Mud Map Example of the Orange dots on my road atlas

Much to my delight I also discovered, "Lodging in France's Monasteries", also by Eileen Barish. Now armed with these 2 volumes, I set about working out an itinerary and where possible, booked nights in the monasteries, abbeys, convents and retreat houses which were listed in my source books, and were in reasonable proximity to my orange dots in the atlases.

Many emails and phone calls followed, and the big challenge, was to correspond in French with those in France. Eileen's book did contain a form letter, but at times my good old school French was called upon heavily to actually make the bookings. Eventually I had a good chunk of reservations, which largely set my itinerary. You can't imagine my joy, every time I received a positive reply, especially to the French respondents. On one occasion I received a three-page reply from a monastery, which was written in French, and initially I misunderstood it, which made me believe that I'd sent them the wrong email accidentally! However, on closer scrutiny, I realized that they were accepting my request for a booking!

Leaving a couple of days without any accommodation booked towards the end of the UK leg for contingencies, I was then able to book rental cars, now knowing where I wanted to pick up and leave them.

Being a practical individual, I understood that trying to both navigate and drive in foreign countries to the many and frequently obscure villages would be very difficult if not impossible, without stopping frequently to get my bearings and check directions. There was nothing for it but to use a GPS.

As I was not returning the hire cars to the pickup location, I was not able to hire GPS units with the cars, and trying to buy appropriate software for my own domestic model was expensive. The solution came through E Bay where I purchased a GPS unit with "world maps", fairly inexpensively, which I hoped would work, but the super sized atlases came along for the ride just in case!

So it was that armed with a copy of The Newmarch Pedigree and other related documents, my French dictionary and phrase book, a sketchbook and art materials, and of course my digital camera in my luggage, I flew out of Australia bound for England.

I need to explain that for practical reasons, even though The Newmarch Pedigree begins in France, I visited England and Wales first, and whilst there, I visited places named in The Newmarch Pedigree as I found them en route and not necessarily chronologically. This is further complicated because the stories of various branches of the family tree which are discussed in The Newmarch Pedigree, run concurrently in different locations. I can however promise, that I will faithfully cite the references and page numbers, which relate to the places I visited in order to share the amazing experiences which I enjoyed on this fantastic journey as they happened.

Chapter II

Having spent 4 days in Abu Dhabi en route, in an effort to break up the jet lag, I arrived at Heathrow airport on 30th September 2011 at around 1pm on a clear blue day, which according to the weather man on the car radio, was the hottest September 30th on record at 29.2 degrees Celsius.

I wasted no time in picking up the little black Peugeot 107 assigned to me and plugged in my budget GPS – nothing! Cheap useless thing! It had crossed my mind more than once that it was perhaps too good to be true! Never mind, I had my super sized Great Britain atlas and having cleared the ring road at Heathrow, I confidently headed off into the heavy pre weekend freeway traffic and managed to go south instead of north!

Some miles later I was able to exit and turn around, and having decided to avoid London completely, made for my first night's destination at Cropthorne in Worcestershire. The countryside was lush and beautiful with green hills interspersed by groves of woodland. There seemed to be such a buzz of excitement as I passed through busy quaint villages of stone and thatched houses, that I thought it must be a long weekend.

After becoming lost a couple of times, some kind locals directed me over a narrow rickety bridge into the village of Cropthorne, where I could see the square tower of a Norman church and then a collection of quaint 16th and 17th century Tudor style thatched houses leaning into the narrow roadway.

Edging my way down Kennel Lane, I arrived at a magnificent 'chocolate box' thatched Tudor house set on 3 acres above the Avon River in manicured gardens complete with a croquet court and mature trees. This was 'Holland House', a retreat house owned by the Anglican Diocese of Worcester, and my base for my first two nights in England.

I could barely believe my good fortune as I rang the doorbell of this magnificent house and was greeted warmly by Shirley, a friendly youngish South African woman who showed me to my room and then informed me that I would be the only guest that night. She then gave me a tour of the historic house, which made me feel as if I was in something from 'Escape to the Country'!

We wandered through the library, drawing room and the amazing dining room with its wood paneling and low dark stained oak beams supported by huge square oak posts. A proper 'Inglenook' fireplace fitted with cosy seats and pretty blue and white tiled walls completed the dining room. All the furniture complemented the age and style of the house.

The old dark stained wooden floorboards, over which Persian carpets were scattered, and the staircase to the first floor where my room was located, creaked and groaned under foot. From my comfortable and spacious room, I overlooked part of the thatch roof and the flagstone courtyard below between the front door and the garden. Shirley told me that I would be alone in the house that night, as she lived in a small cottage at the bottom of the garden, and the other booked guests had failed to arrive.

Beautiful "Holland House"

I sat in the wonderful old dining room while Shirley served me a magnificent 3-course meal, which had been prepared by the cook:

* Hot spicy tomato soup
* A very plump piece of chicken wrapped in bacon, with side dishes of carrots, broccoli and potato bake
* Finally a huge apple Charlotte tart and cream which even I couldn't finish.

I persuaded Shirley to join me for the last course and coffee as I realized that she was sitting alone in the kitchen eating her meal, and so we enjoyed chatting for a couple of hours.

After a good sleep, I woke early to a perfect morning and took a stroll around the beautiful village before being served a great English breakfast with 'the works'. Realizing that I really did need the GPS, I took another look at it, and once I had set it to 'United Kingdom', it worked perfectly! It's amazing what a sleep will do for you!

With the GPS set for Gloucester Cathedral, I headed off on the forty minute or so trip.

Inglenook Fireplace in Holland House

Chapter III

The Newmarch Pedigree reads as follows: Page 3

"He (Bernard) was also a benefactor to the Monastery at Gloucester, to which he gave, Temp. 2 W. 2, (in the second year of the reign of King William 11), A.D. 1088, the manor and advowson of Glasbury, Co. Brecon, with the tythes of other parishes in the counties of Brecon and Hereford, some of which belong to the See of Gloucester to this day.

Bernard was buried beneath the cloisters of the Cathedral, with other eminent persons, whose names Leland informs us were in his time, A.D.1550, painted on the wall of the Chapter House near the graves in black letter. *This statement has been since verified by the discovery of the inscriptions themselves in 1858, when the Chapter House was restored, and the accumulated whitewash of centuries removed. On the North wall in a niche can now be traced: -*

"hic jacet Rogerus Comes de Hereford"
On the South wall in another niche: -
"Hic jacet Bernardus De Novo Mercato."
"Hic jacet Paganus De Cadurcis."
And in an adjoining panel: -
"Hic jacet Robart Cortus."
"Hic jacet Adam De Cadurcis."

(Camden's Brit by Gibson, 707-9. Dugd. Baronage 1. 435.
Jones's Brecknock; Thoroton's Notts; Collinson's Somerset; Leland's M.S.S.)

My fabulous GPS, now affectionately known as "George", made my life ever so easy in navigating me to the amazing Gloucester Cathedral on this beautiful October 1st Saturday morning. After parking in the council car park, I walked through the ancient streets, many of the old buildings leaning sideways or outwards into the main street.

I was nervous with anticipation as I approached the enormous Cathedral. Would the evidence be still there? It was nearly 1,000 years old, and the source material was almost 150 years old!

My mission was twofold:

- To find where Bernard was buried beneath the cloisters
- To find the inscription in the Chapter House.

A very kind lady volunteer welcomed visitors in the porch area of the Cathedral. I told her of the reason for my visit and she told me I needed to find one of the volunteers who were wearing red sashes. A very old man fitted the bill. He told me that some high school A Level Students were setting up a display of their work in the Chapter House, and didn't think I'd be allowed to go in! – But that he'd take me there anyway!

We cut through the beautiful cloister and soon arrived at the Chapter House, which was part of the original monastery. I told my guide that I was looking for an inscription on the South Wall. He said, "Well good luck"!

We arrived at the door to be told by, an 'important' parent or teacher that we couldn't enter. I explained that I'd come from Australia for this, and just kept moving forward and looking up to my left, I saw an inscription in an alcove. Looking to my right, I looked up, and just as George and Charles Newmarch had quoted, there was the inscription in black letters:

"*Hic jacet Bernardus De Novo Mercato*".

I was so excited and the old guide was stunned! I just needed a couple of photos now but somebody's blue mosaic plate work of art was in Bernard's niche! I asked one of the 'important' people if the plate could be removed for a moment, but none of the first five or six people were 'important' or courageous enough to lift the plate! Finally the headmaster gave the go ahead for the momentary lifting of the school artwork, after I explained again that I'd come half way round the world for this.

Jubilant at having found and photographed the inscription, I now needed to find where Bernard was buried. The cloisters are the covered walkways, which lie between the sizeable square courtyard and the enclave of cathedral buildings. The huge and majestic ornate stone vault of the cloister is an intricate fan design and apparently featured in at least one of the Harry Potter films. I believe that the cloister was a place of meditation for the monks, who sat and contemplated in booths along the cloister, or as they walked daily over the burial stones which lay in the stone paving.

I asked my red sashed guide, (who was now taking me a little more seriously), if there was a plan or map detailing who was buried where. "No" he replied, "you'll just have to go and look"! I thanked him for his help and began

Cloisters of Gloucester Cathedral

*Inscription in the Chapter House of Gloucester Cathedral, and the
offending Blue Mosaic Plate!*

27

Bernard de Novo Mercato's Inscriptiom on the Chapter House Wall

Possible burial stone of Bernard de Novo Mercato

the painstaking task of studying every burial stone for clues.

A thousand years is a long time and many of the stones were worn smooth giving no indication of who lay beneath them. I spent quite some time assiduously scanning each stone for any clue, which might indicate that Bernard lay beneath. I reached one stone that was a little rough looking, and noticed that at one end, there was a circular depression, which having just drawn the family coat of arms, I recognized as a knight's head. Then I could see the plumes, and then the shield complete with diamond shapes! This was very exciting! This must be Bernard!

I found one of "The Friends of Gloucester Cathedral", who, on seeing my drawing of the family crest, concurred, and joined in my jubilation. Although this is purely speculative, I was very content with the find, and all this before lunch too!

I left the Cathedral feeling ecstatic. Recently I have read of another possibility raised by Christopher Daniell in his book, "Death and Burial in Medieval England, 1066-1550", which throws up the possibility that sometimes unmarked graves in the cloisters, "would also have had wall markers either nearby or elsewhere in the church". And, further, he cites Payne & Payne, 1994), "in Gloucester Cathedral chapter house, eight names were painted on the walls as memorials". Bernard was one of these eight, so whether I had found his burial stone complete with family coat of arms, or he lay beneath an unmarked stone, I can't say.

Buoyed by my success at the Cathedral, I stepped out

into the hottest October day in history at 29.9 degrees Celsius. Take away English fish and chips with salt and vinegar from the Gloucester chippy was great as I headed off to Cirencester.

Cirencester is a medieval market town in the heart of the Cotswolds and is characterized by a prominent market place, narrow winding lanes and ancient buildings. The reason for my visit is that one of the authors of 𝕿𝖍𝖊 𝕹𝖊𝖜𝖒𝖆𝖗𝖈𝖍 𝕻𝖊𝖉𝖎𝖌𝖗𝖊𝖊, has signed off:
Geo. Fred. Newmarch, Cirencester. January 1868. He is also found in the 1881 England Census, at 12 Sheep Street, Cirencester, 'Retired Solicitor'.

"George", the GPS, (now my best friend), directed me to 12 Sheep Street. Unfortunately, number 12 no longer exists, and a row of modern housing units occupies the site. A search at the history section of the local library failed to bring to light any street number changes, which may have occurred over the years.

I did however find that there is a Roman archeological site in the heart of town and I have subsequently discovered that Chas. H. Newmarch, the co-author of 𝕿𝖍𝖊 𝕹𝖊𝖜𝖒𝖆𝖗𝖈𝖍 𝕻𝖊𝖉𝖎𝖌𝖗𝖊𝖊, has co-authored a book entitled, ""Illustrations of the Remains of Roman Art in Cirencester, the Site of Antient Corinium", by Prof. Buckman and C.H. Newmarch. Signed Cirencester 10th June 1850.

After a pleasant walk around the meandering streets, I moved on to Burford, Oxfordshire, the birthplace of:
George Frederick Newmarch Baptized: 17/9/1817
John Newmarch　　　　　　Baptized: 14/8/1822

Charles Henry Newmarch   Baptized: 06/8/1824
These 3 brothers were the sons of Mary and George Newmarch, from York; George (their father), having been baptized at Holy Trinity Mickelgate, York, on 07/1//1791. Sadly John died as an infant at three and a half months of age on 23/11/1822 at Burford.

Burford, is a picturesque village, marked by Cotswold stone cottages dating to the 16th century, and is a popular tourist destination. I enjoyed wandering around in search of any clues about the family, and soaking up the atmosphere. The main street, which runs downhill, was jammed with tourists on this beautiful, unseasonally warm day.

I made my way down to the historic parish church, but on that lazy Saturday afternoon, found no signs of the Newmarches on this quick visit, so, I headed back to Holland House where I was again warmly greeted by Shirley who informed me that the other expected guests still hadn't arrived, and so we enjoyed a pleasant evening together again, eating a wonderful dinner and sharing experiences.

Chapter IV

Next morning, I bade farewell to Shirley and Holland House and headed east to Wales. The day was again magnificent as I drove through picturesque, lush countryside, green and treed and dotted with ancient castles. It was Sunday, and I came across Abergavenny, another ancient market town, which has a very large market hall where an African fair was in full swing, complete with drums and singing!

I pushed on to Brecon through wooded valleys and hills rising into mountains, the seat of Bernard de Neufmarche's, (Newmarch's) power, viz: The Newmarch Pedigree Page 2

"On the death of William 1, (The Conqueror), and when his followers overran the realm, in Temp. Rufus, (William 11), A.D. 1087, Bernard invaded Brecknockshire, and having routed and slain Bleddyn ap Maenarch, gained possession of the greater part of that province. He established himself at Brecon, where he built his castle....."

While planning the trip, I discovered that the remains of Bernard's castle, built in A.D. 1093, are today part of "The Brecon Castle Hotel"! Unbelievable! So I hastened to book in for a night, wondering what I might find in the evidential trail.

My excitement and anticipation mounted as I neared Brecon, which is nestled in the valley at the base of the Brecon Beacons and in the heart of The Brecon Beacons National Park. The town is now a tourist hub and a base for those enjoying hiking, camping and other outdoor pursuits.

I drove through the narrow winding streets to the confluence of the Honddu and Usk Rivers, and there, towering above, on the top of a rocky outcrop were the ancient stonewall fortifications of Bernard de Neufmarche's castle and the Brecon Castle Hotel.

I felt almost breathless at the sight, and followed the winding road up to the Hotel Car Park and the hotel reception, which is in the newer building, probably built in the 16th or 17th century, and according to Edward Parry of Christchurch College, Brecon, the Morgan family of Tredegar Park renovated it in 1809. (Brecon Castle Hotel Website).

I checked in, feeling flushed with excitement and brightly explained to the receptionist my connection with Bernard de Neufmarche and the castle. She obviously had no idea what I was talking about and stared at me blankly as if she was dealing with a mad woman!

Feeling somewhat deflated and possibly fraudulent, I sheepishly climbed the stairs to my room, which was in the attic with dark stained, oak beams over head, and like the bulk of the Hotel was contained within the newer building. Unfortunately only one wall of the original castle is part of the Hotel, that being the wall of the bar adjacent to the ballroom.

Throwing myself on the bed, I picked up the Castle Hotel information folder, which contained, "A Brief Historical Guide to the Castle", and scanning the document, my mood lifted as I read, *"Brecon Castle and town is Norman in origin. The castle came first and was the creation of Bernard de*

My first view of Bernard's Castle

Neufmarche, the brother of William the Conqueror"! Yes! Some validation!

It was 3.00pm on Sunday afternoon, and the Information Folder explained that Evensong was on at the Cathedral at 3.30pm. I was tired but decided to go. Whilst driving into town earlier, I had been looking for any sign of The Parish Church of St John the Evangelist, without success because of this reference:

𝕿𝖍𝖊 𝕹𝖊𝖜𝖒𝖆𝖗𝖈𝖍 𝕻𝖊𝖉𝖎𝖌𝖗𝖊𝖊 page 3

"At Brecon, in Temp. Henry 1, circ. A.D.1100, Bernard, at the instance of his confessor, Roger, a Monk of Battle, founded a Benedictine Priory, which he liberally endowed and constituted a cell to Battle Abbey, in memory of his first wife Agnes. The Priory Church is still remaining, and is the principal Parish Church of Brecon, dedicated to St. John the Evangelist, to whom Bernard had dedicated his Priory. Part of the original Norman building may still be traced." (Dugd. Monast. 3. 259-263)

The Cathedral wasn't, far, but as I was short of time and didn't really know where I was going, I took the car, and arriving at the Cathedral Car Park, I looked up and read: "The Cathedral Church of St. John the Evangelist"! I could barely believe my eyes and muttered a prayer of thanks as I walked through the lych-gate and into the vast Cathedral.

The befrocked Cathedral Choir of fifteen to twenty souls, was already in full voice, and three clergy officiated at the service, and having grown up in the Anglican Church in Sydney, I was familiar with the liturgy.

The Cathedral Church of St. John the Evangelist Brecon as viewed from the car park.

Being a cathedral, the space was enormous and the pomp and ceremony, befitting; however the congregation of ten people was disappointing.

At the completion of the service, I approached the tall clergyman in the gold robe, and introduced myself as a descendant of Bernard de Neufmarche. "You've come to pay the bills, have you?" He chortled. I was very relieved that he actually knew about Bernard, unlike the young hotel receptionist. He introduced himself as Geoffrey Marshall, Dean of the Cathedral! "Your ancestor built this place, come and see some of what there is left to see". He strode off down through the length of the Cathedral, his gold robes flowing behind, and me in his wake.

We stopped abruptly just shy of the choir stalls on the left of the sanctuary. In front of us was a pew divided down the centre into two wide seats. On the top of the back stood three carved wooden knights, one at each end, and one in the centre. They were each, 15-18inches high, and each one was named below his feet.

On the left was NEWMARCH, in the centre was (King) William 1 Reg., and on the right Sir John Scull. This was quite exciting. Strangely though, the pew was "dedicated to the memory of Bernard Newmarch, builder of the second priory: William 1. Reg. and of his companion Sir John Scull." Crouching lions were the armrests, and blue tapestry cushions softened the seat. I'm unsure where the reference to the second priory comes from or who Sir John Scull was, however the pew was "The gift of William Ellis Scull Philadelphia USA".

Wooden Pew Carving of Bernard de Neufmarche in Brecon Cathedral

The Pew in Brecon Cathedral with carvings

Geoffrey invited me to follow him to the vestry, where a woman lifted the heavy gold vestment from his shoulders. He told me that there had been an architectural survey of the Cathedral, under a 'Royal Commission on the Ancient and Historical Monuments of Wales'. He started searching for a copy of the document, and indeed, enlisted the help of anyone who entered the room. Eventually satisfaction beamed across his face as he extracted a glossy book from a dark corner.

"To Wendy, from Geoffrey (Dean), 2/X/11", he inscribed, and then presented it to me, but not before bringing my attention to page 5 which reads, "*THE HISTORY OF THE PRIORY*" "*The priory of St. John the Evangelist, Brecon, was founded by Bernard de Neufmarche at the end of the 11th century, shortly after his defeat of Rhys ap Tewdwr, King of Brycheiniog, at Brecon in 1093. He gave "the Church of St. John the Evangelist near his castle at Brecon, together with 'a certain property called The Old Town', to the newly founded Benedictine Abbey of Battle at the request of one of his followers, a Monk of Battle named Roger*".

At that moment, Peter, the Cathedral's resident historian, walked into the room. He apparently was responsible for turning 'the tithing barn' into The Heritage Centre. On hearing of the reason for my visit, he produced a very old book from his pocket on the history of Brecon.

Unfortunately I failed to note the title or author, but Peter read me some excerpts which detailed some of the character traits of Bernard and his knights, portraying

The Tithing Barn inside the Brecon Cathedral Walls

The Brecon Castle Hotel

them to be cavalier and ruthless, and that to make amends for his actions, Bernard built the Benedictine Priory, and lavished gifts upon the monks! Peter then chastised the Dean for giving away a book, saying that they sell for six pounds in the shop, which Geoffrey laughed off as "needing to get rid of them somehow"!

Geoffrey had such a bubbly personality, and although he said he wouldn't be there, invited me to return to the Cathedral the next day to see 'the tithing barn' and the remnant of the priory, and other buildings in the Cathedral complex. I was elated as I returned to the Hotel, after such a positive and unexpected experience.

As there was plenty of daylight left, I walked down to the river to survey the castle from a distance. It gave me goose bumps to be there. It is thought that Bernard chose that site for the castle partly because of the rivers, which were useful for defence, and to drive the mills. There were no bridges then, but fords across the Usk were important links for the Normans. Apparently the upstream ford is still known as 'Rhynd Bernard'. (Brecon Castle Hotel Website).

From the hotel dining room that evening, looking across the hotel lawns and pink hollyhocks in the gardens, was Brecon, nestled in the valley before the rising green presence of the Brecon Beacons. I marvelled again that I was able to share in this remnant of history.

Next morning, I enjoyed the view once more along with my ham and eggs for breakfast, checked out, and then headed downtown.

A Side Door at Brecon Cathedral

At Brecon Museum, I found more references to Bernard before making my way to the Cathedral.

I was particularly interested in 'the tithing barn', firstly, from a Scriptural point of view, where in Malachi 3:10 the Israelites are commanded to "bring the whole tithe into the storehouse" (New International Version), and then this previously mentioned reference in 𝕮𝖍𝖊 𝕹𝖊𝖜𝖒𝖆𝖗𝖈𝖍 𝕻𝖊𝖉𝖎𝖌𝖗𝖊𝖊, 𝕻𝖆𝖌𝖊 3: *"He (Bernard) was also a benefactor to the Monastery at Gloucester, to which he gave, Temp. 2 W. 2, (the second year of the reign of William 11), A.D. 1088, the manor and advowson of Glasbury, Co. Brecon, with the tythes of other parishes in the counties of Brecon and Hereford, some of which belong to the See of Gloucester to this day."*

The tithe is one tenth of one's income, which is to be given back to God. In Bible times and indeed in Bernard's time, the tithe portion was given in kind, in crops of wheat or barley or sheep etc., so hence the need for the tithing barn, (or storehouse), to store the produce. The tithe was, and still is given by the parishioners to support the clergy of their parish.

Discovering that there was a 'tithing barn' was an unexpected and poignant visual lesson, which one may possibly only understand by being physically present.

Today the tithing barn at the Cathedral has been turned into the Heritage Centre, which also has references to Bernard. Whilst there, I found out that 'the Roll of Battle Abbey', is kept at the Abbey at Battle.

The Newmarch Pedigree Page 1 states: *"His (Bernard), name appears on the roll of Battle Abbey, and he was one of the witnesses to King William's Charter to the Monks of Battle. (Dugd. Monast. 1, 317). A facsimile of his signature is given in (the Autographic Mirror, Vol. 2 No. 20".*

Whilst I was chatting with a volunteer at the centre, she mentioned that 'Battle' was a place just out of Brecon! Off I headed, out into the rolling hills, scanning every inch of the countryside for an abbey. I reached 'Battle' ten minutes or so later, but no sign of any abbey. The small hamlet had several houses, a few farm cottages, and St Cynog's Church, Parish of Battle. I walked through the graveyard which surrounded the rather dilapidated stone church, looking for any clue, without success, so I made my way back through the township of Brecon to Llangasty Retreat House, where I would spend the next two nights.

Chapter V

Llangasty Retreat House, which belongs to the Anglican Dioceses of Swansea, Brecon and Llandaff, is found 20 minutes or so to the south east of Brecon. After leaving the main road, one turns into a narrow country lane, which winds through verdant pastures and hedgerows of the Welsh Hills, then down towards Llangorse Lake through avenues of mature oak trees on the descent.

Turning into the driveway, the handsome bluestone, two-storey building could be seen at the end of the paving, standing, dignified, and overlooking the lake across emerald green fields. I felt truly blest once more to be coming to such a beautiful place.

I was greeted warmly and told that a small retreat group would also be coming in, and in fact they started arriving as I did. They introduced themselves straight away and invited me to join with them in any or all of their sessions.

At afternoon tea, I learned that the group of about ten people from various parishes in the south of England had been coming there every year, for seven years.

Llangasty was built originally around 1870, as the Rectory and Vicarage for St Gastyn's Church, whose spire one could see through the tops of the trees at the lake's edge. St Gastyn's was built in 1848 by Robert Raikes on the site of an ancient church built by a 5th century hermit named Gastyn, who was later beatified. Robert Raikes' grand daughter, Miss Dorothy Raikes, was responsible for keeping

The Front Door of Llangasty House

Llangasty as a place of spiritual service, and in fact personally purchased the property in 1947 and made it available as a retreat house, thus continuing the Raikes' family's long devotion to the work of the church in the local parish.

Curious about St. Gastyn's, I decided to take a walk down there before dinner. As I approached, I could see another beautiful gabled stone building adjacent to the church. I walked through the substantial lych-gate, and arriving at the church porch, found a lady preparing flowers.

It was Harvest Festival time, and people everywhere were decorating their churches with the fruits of their labours, with fruit and flowers, sheaves of wheat and barley and other produce.

I spoke to the lady who was probably in her late 60's, or perhaps a little more, I can't say. We chatted briefly, before I commented on the beautiful stone building next door, and asked if she knew if it had once been the church. She replied that it had been built as the schoolhouse, "and I'm lucky enough to live there"! I asked her name, and she replied, "I'm Rosemary Raikes". I was amazed, and realized that it was her great grandfather who had built the church and the school!

I then told her that I was a direct descendant of Bernard Newmarch, then she was 'blown away', and said "there is so much history about him around here". She told me that I must go to 'Hay-on-Wye', which is a town of bookshops, and buy the book, "Lady of Hay" by Barbara Erskine. She said, "It's fictional but it's all about your

Brecon Cathedral Stone Baptismal Font believed to be from the Original Abbey

ancestor!" I thanked her and returned to Llangasty marvelling again at how the way was being opened up for me.

We sat at dinner at a long refractory table, looking out over the grazing cattle to the lake and the hills beyond. I sat next to Anthea, such a lovely lady from Somerset. She told me that she was half Australian, but that she had been born in India as her father was working there. She then told me the sad story of her mother dying there when she drowned after fainting into a bath, which had been run for her by a servant. This occurred at Ooty, when Anthea was only eighteen months old.

I told her that I was at Lushington School in Ooty, (Ootacamund) for seven and a half months in the seventies. At that moment, Malcolm, the Anglican minister in the group, (who was sitting opposite me), said, "What year were you at Lushington? I was teaching there in 1972"! I told him that I was there in 1973, and it happened that we knew most of the same people! How amazing!

Whilst still at the dinner table, I nonchalantly commented to Anthea that I had been to 'Battle' today.

Her reply was, "I went to school at Battle Abbey". This surely couldn't be happening! "Where is Battle Abbey?" I asked amazed. She told me that it was at 'Battle', near Hastings, in Sussex, and it was the site where the 'Battle of Hastings' actually took place! She told me that the castle was there and that you could walk around the battlefield and see the abbey. Now I knew why I had left a couple of days free in the itinerary!

I joined with the group for their evening session followed by prayers in the chapel. What an incredible day. This was only the third day of my quest and already so much had happened.

After a good night's sleep, I joined in early prayers again and after breakfast together, set 'George' for Hay-on-Wye, and was directed right around Llangorse Lake, through narrow winding country lanes and idyllic farms. En route, I passed a sign to 'Glasbury', which I remembered seeing in 𝕿𝖍𝖊 𝕹𝖊𝖜𝖒𝖆𝖗𝖈𝖍 𝕻𝖊𝖉𝖎𝖌𝖗𝖊𝖊.

The day was cooler, and a little misty as I arrived in Hay-on-Wye, Herefordshire. The streets were filled with secondhand bookshops; twenty-nine, I counted on the brochure, and two bookbinders. Hay Castle rose behind the main street, imposing itself on the landscape. Since my visit, I have discovered that Hay Castle was probably built by William Revel, one of Bernard de Newmarch's knights, (Jeffrey L. Thomas, 1999 in his article on Hay Castle).

I began my search for 'Lady of Hay', engaging in conversation with the shopkeepers as I went. One lady, who didn't have a copy of the book I was looking for, thought that it may be difficult to find, but recommended the shops, which she thought I would be most likely to have have success. Yes, Shop 16 on the map, 'The Addyman Annexe' did have a secondhand copy. Just six pounds and ninety-five pence, and the seven hundred and fifty plus page volume, was now in my hand.

Very excitedly I told the story of my quest to the shopkeeper, and that Glasbury was mentioned in my text, that 𝕿𝔥𝔢 𝕹𝔢𝔴𝔪𝔞𝔯𝔠𝔥 𝕻𝔢𝔡𝔦𝔤𝔯𝔢𝔢, page 3, inferred that Bernard had a manor at Glasbury, and that he sent the tithes from there to Gloucester. She told me that she thought there was a castle at Glasbury!

I made my way to the Tourist Information office, to find out if they knew anything of that castle at Glasbury. The lady on duty kindly 'Googled' it for me, and came up with a full page print out, entitled "Glasbury Castle", which showed that the land (including Glasbury), which pertained to Gloucester Abbey had been granted by Bernard de Neufmarche before 1088. It went on to say that the castle had been destroyed, probably in the 13th century by warring lords, but that, "the centre and west side of the castle mound could still seen beside the access road into a cul-de-sac behind the 'Lamb Inn'". (Details supplied by Clwyd-Powis Archaeological Trust).

With this information in hand, I made my way to Glasbury, a 'green village', so the sign said, on the River Wye. I saw an imposing manor house estate called 'Glasbury House', (which is now an outdoor activity centre), and drove in to enquire as to the whereabouts of the 'Lamb Inn'. The office ladies in the rather grand two storey mansion, were very helpful and supplied me with more print outs, and the directions to the 'The Lamb Inn'. They also volunteered, that there was a Newmarch Street in Brecon!

I headed back down the long driveway through park-like grounds, and found my way to 'The Lamb Inn', which almost seemed to be sitting in the old moat, partly below ground level. I took some photos, and whilst walking

Bookshops in Hay-on-Wye

around, found part of the old castle wall complete with arrow slots. I then took my leave of this quiet village, and headed back to Brecon, where I found and photographed Newmarch Street, then had afternoon tea, at Bernard's Cathedral.

At Llangasty, my friends told me over a delicious roast chicken dinner, that they would have no evening session that night, as there was a Harvest Festival Service on at St. Gastyn's at 7.30pm. It was a very colourful and happy service, and the obscure country church was packed. At the end of the service, the organist started to play a hymn as a recessional. No one moved, but everyone stood there and broke into spontaneous singing. This continued for three or four hymns, then everyone laughed and chatted and finally, reluctantly filed out of the church, much to the relief of the two clergymen who were waiting at the door to shake hands with the congregation as they left!

The happy day ended with hot chocolate and chatter back at Llangasty.

Chapter VI

We shared morning prayers in the chapel, before enjoying breakfast together. We then made our fond farewells, with plenty of hugs and kisses and lovely cards being given to me by Anthea and Chris, who, said that she'd woken up feeling as if she'd known me for years, and yet it was but two nights. I felt the same way. It had been a wonderful time, but now I was heading northeast, to Leicestershire.

En route, I fortuitously saw a sign to Kenilworth, which I recalled having seen in The Newmarch Pedigree. So my first stop became Kenilworth Castle, where Adam de Newmarch, (six generations from Bernard through his first wife, Agnes), was involved in the siege of Kenilworth in 1266. Leading up to this, The Newmarch Pedigree, page 10, tells us, *"This Adam was a man of great note in the Reign of Henry 111, and took an active and conspicuous part in the proceedings of those troublous times, having been one of the barons summoned in 42 Henry 111, (1259), to attend the King with horse and arms at Chester, and afterwards one of those in 47 Henry 111, (1264), who advanced his banner in open rebellion against the King at Northampton, where he and others were taken prisoner. His manors of Bentley, Wymersley, Campsall, and Thorne, Co. York, and all his lands in the county of Lincoln were then seized under the King's warrant, and committed to the charge of Richard Foliat."*

In 1264, discontent against the King spilled over into civil war, and the barons led by Simon de Montfort, (who in

1253 was granted Kenilworth Castle for life), defeated and imprisoned the King, as stated in 𝕿𝖍𝖊 𝕹𝖊𝖜𝖒𝖆𝖗𝖈𝖍 𝕻𝖊𝖉𝖎𝖌𝖗𝖊𝖊 𝕻𝖆𝖌𝖊 10: *"On the defeat of the royalists at Lewes, where the King with the Prince and the chief nobles who adhered to him were captured, Adam de Newmarch was once more summoned to parliament, and further troubles ensued"*,

The 'further troubles', was the Great Siege of 1266 at Kenilworth Castle, where the barons and their knights, held the King and his royal forces at bay in apparently one of the few full-scale medieval sieges on English soil, which was the longest, and lasted for 6 months. Eventually the remnant of the garrison, who were by then decimated by starvation and disease, surrendered under favourable terms, when a parliament summoned by Henry 111, on a piece of land near the castle, resulted in the 'Dictum of Kenilworth'.

𝕿𝖍𝖊 𝕹𝖊𝖜𝖒𝖆𝖗𝖈𝖍 𝕻𝖊𝖉𝖎𝖌𝖗𝖊𝖊, 𝕻𝖆𝖌𝖊 11, confirms this, *" his party was again defeated at Kenilworth, he obtained restitution of his estates under the 'Dictum of Kenilworth', though probably under conditions for the control of his power, and the deprivation of his son in favour of his daughter and her issue, which were afterwards carried into effect"*.

So here I was at the site of an amazing piece of history. Mostly in ruins now, the castle is still a substantial presence on the hill. One can only imagine how magnificent it was when the 'mere', an immense artificial lake, which surrounded the castle at the time of the siege, existed.

It was primarily built as a defence, but also provided a source of fish and waterfowl, and was boated upon by the King.

The Ruins of Kenilworth Castle

I took my leave of Kenilworth, contemplating what an unexpected and significant visit that was. I made my way to Leicester, and made a beeline for Montgomerey's, the oldest manufacturer of duffle coats in the UK.

As I had arrived at the factory, and announced to the receptionist that I'd come from Australia to buy one of their duffle coats, an amused but very polite English gentleman, (probably the manager), told me that this was a little irregular as he handed me an orange safety vest, and led me into the warehouse.

There I was confronted by thousands of duffle coats, individually covered in plastic and hanging in endless rows, in multitudes of colours and sizes. I selected one in navy blue, with check lining, antler toggles, adjustable hood, and deep pockets. The warm heavy, familiar coat, was just like the one which I'd bought in Edinburgh 40 years ago. Delighted with my purchase, I continued on my way to 'Launde Abbey', my accommodation for the next two nights.

Chapter VII

'Launde Abbey' is a beautiful Tudor/Elizabethan manor house, which is now an Anglican Retreat and Conference Centre, and belongs to the Diocese of Leicester. It nestles at the base of grassy hills, in 440 acres of an idyllic farmland estate, about 20 miles or so from Leicester, and a million miles from care. As one approaches over the crest of the hill, on the narrow, single-track lane, the vision of the manor house is particularly impressive, and imposing on the landscape.

The rambling mansion, complemented by a large converted Georgian stable block and 10 acres of manicured gardens, was much larger in every way than any of the other retreat houses I had stayed in to that point.

The car park was full and overflowing on to the grass verge, and I probably walked past 40 to 50 cars, on my way to Reception. David welcomed me and showed me to my room, which was located in the main house. It was enormous, with 14-foot ceilings, a sofa as well as two king single beds, and a huge en suite bathroom. The room was right in the middle of the house and the tall windows directly overlooked the formal gardens.

Again, I was so blessed. At afternoon tea I met 14 or 15 women who had come together for a week, purely to patchwork. They were accommodated in the Old Stable block, and had been given a huge room, which was set up with tables. There they had plenty of room for their sewing machines, and to spread out and admire their work.

Impression of a Beautiful Sculpture seen at Launde Abbey.

There were individuals having 'silent' retreats, and a Catholic group from the Stella Maris Mission to Seamen who were from England and Ireland, and amongst their number, was an Australian Nun. These folk very kindly invited me to join them for dinner. Launde Abbey has beautifully elegant public rooms, including the library, and other 'salons', which are used as conference rooms.

Attached to the main house, there is also a Renaissance chapel, which has stunning, medieval stained glass windows. The chapel in fact, is the only remnant of the original priory church that was established by a group of Augustinian canons in 1119 A.D. on the site. The priory church was closed down by Thomas Cromwell in the 1530's as part of the 'Dissolution', however Cromwell took a liking to Launde Abbey, and commissioned the building of the mansion but he never lived there as he was executed for treason!

That evening before dinner, I went to evening prayers at 'The Emmaus Chapel'. This is a small, whitewashed stone building behind the stable block, and could easily be mistaken for the garden or tool shed! Six of us, and the Minister filled the small musty space. There was room for no more as the Evening Prayers were said.

Following a good night's sleep, and a gourmet bacon and egg breakfast, I headed off on a crisp, clear day to Belton, which was actually back over the hill and only 5 or 10 minutes away through farmland and hedgerows. En route, several pheasants played 'chicken' with my front wheels, but somehow managed to survive! – I think!

Charles Henry Newmarch, co-author of 𝕿𝖍𝖊 𝕹𝖊𝖜𝖒𝖆𝖗𝖈𝖍 𝕻𝖊𝖉𝖎𝖌𝖗𝖊𝖊, signed off on page vii of the Preface thus:

"Chas. H. Newmarch,

Belton Vicarage, Uppingham.

January 1868."

I drove into Belton, near Uppingham, in Rutland, which distinguishes itself by being the smallest County in England. Belton is a sleepy village in the hills, quite distant from anywhere, especially one hundred and fifty years ago. One can only imagine the difficulties involved in undertaking research in 1868, with no such tools as the Internet, telephone or even easy access to a library. One imagines long nights sitting by candlelight with quill and ink bottle, writing long letters of enquiry, then afterwards, mounting a horse and riding tedious distances, to visit those holding information about the Newmarches.

My GPS, (George), in taking me to 'town centre', conveniently and invariably, directed me to the parish church, which is usually where I needed to be, as the case was in Belton. The Parish Church of St Peter stood on the high side of the village square. The early morning was fresh but clear as I alighted from the car in my new duffle coat, wondering if the once stately building, to the left of the church, which was currently empty and under repair, was in fact the old vicarage.

As I stood musing on the deserted square, a gentleman appeared through a gateway opposite and approached, wondering if he could help the 'lost stranger'. I asked if he knew if the building next to the church was the old vicarage, and told him of my quest to follow in the footsteps of my Newmarch forebears.

He told me that he didn't think that the building was the vicarage, but introduced himself as 'Norman', and invited me into his home as he thought there might have been some information inside, which his wife had collected.

We walked through the cottage garden and into the beautiful thatched cottage (Circa 1500), named 'Martin Haven'. Norman told me that it was the last remaining thatched house in the village, and that until a fire in 1774, the whole village had thatched roofs. As we walked through the low doorways and the living room with its dark stained low ceiling beams, it again made me feel that I had ventured into something out of "Escape to the Country", (an English rural property search TV programme).

We continued through to the conservatory, where he served me coffee, while his two lovely dogs begged to play. He told me of his late wife, (Moira)'s love of local history, and then produced a pile of her notes, which he let me browse. Norman joked about the Aussies beating the 'poms' at football and cricket and asked me to tell them to go easy on them!

One of Moira's pages, showed that Charles Henry Newmarch was the Vicar of St Peter's, Belton, for thirty-seven years, from 1856-1893, and that during that time, in 1870, he built the Church of England School which had approximately forty children enrolled, aged from six to twelve years.

Norman offered to photocopy anything that I thought would be helpful, and then took me over to the church where we found Alan, one of the Church Wardens, mowing. He enthusiastically took me into the church and proudly showed me a beautiful mural, which was a tribute to Charles Henry Newmarch and his wife Annie, who had so faithfully served the people of Belton for thirty-seven years.

Alan went on to say that he thought that two of Charles and Annie's daughters had died as a result of a diphtheria outbreak, during their time in Belton. I later walked through the churchyard and indeed found the gravestones, side by side, and now difficult to read:

"Emily Mary Newmarch, Died 1882 Aged 24 years",

"Geraldine Newmarch, Died 1885 Aged 22 years".

One can only imagine the heartache and pain that the family endured. A third daughter, is mentioned on the memorial plaque in the church, as her mother died at her home, Christ Church Vicarage, Regent's Park London, in 1910.

I believe their son Bernard, was born in Belton in 1858, and immigrated to Australia and practiced as a physician and surgeon in Sydney from at least 1893. It is therefore likely that he was away studying at university at the time of his sisters' deaths.

Alan said, "You must come and meet Audrey, as she knows all about the Newmarchs". So we walked across the road to a house only a few doors along from 'Martin Haven', and were greeted by Phillip, Audrey's husband. Alan went back to mowing the church grounds, and Phillip showed me

Parish Church of St. Peter

Belton in Rutland

Vicars

1574 - 1609	Johes Tokye
1610 - 1638	Francisus Leat
1638 - 1663	Joannes Allington
1664 - 1665	Francis Meres
1666 - 1683	Thomas Stockman
1683 - 1685	Giles Coker
1686 - 1724	Thomas Smith
1724 - 1761	Richard Smith
1762 - 1811	John Wight Wickes
1811 - 1837	N. Graham
1838 - 1856	E. A. Earle
1856 - 1893	Charles Henry Newmarch
1894 - 1909	C. J. Rowland Berkeley
1910 - 1925	George J. Pattison
1926 - 1947	David Michael Evans
1948 - 1949	J. P. Bryant Smith
1950 - 1954	J Jacques — Assistant Curate
1954 - 1957	A. B. Berry — Assistant Curate
1957 - 1960	E Siddall
1962 - 1965	W. Noy
1966 - 1976	Cuthbert Cassen
1977 - 1982	John Smith
1982 - 1999	John Willett
2000 - 2010	Stephen Evans
2011 -	Rachel Watts

October 2011

List of Vicars at St Peter's Belton

Tribute to Rev Charles Henry Newmarch

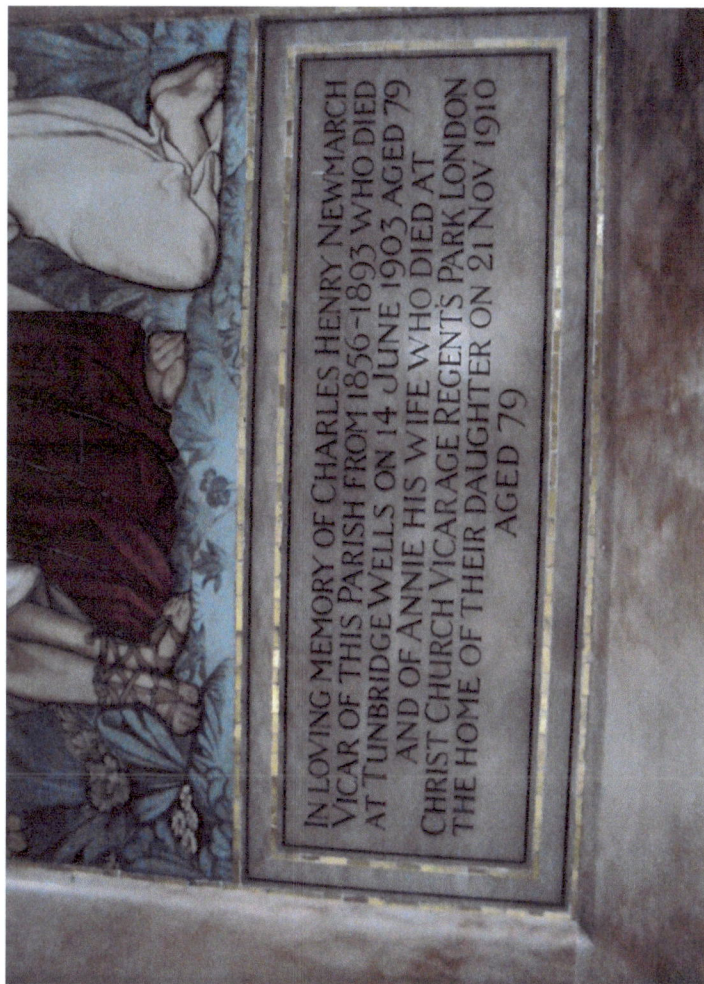

IN LOVING MEMORY OF CHARLES HENRY NEWMARCH
VICAR OF THIS PARISH FROM 1856–1893 WHO DIED
AT TUNBRIDGE WELLS ON 14 JUNE 1903 AGED 79
AND OF ANNIE HIS WIFE WHO DIED AT
CHRIST CHURCH VICARAGE REGENT'S PARK LONDON
THE HOME OF THEIR DAUGHTER ON 21 NOV 1910
AGED 79

Tribute Inscription

Final Resting place of Emily & Geraldine Newmarch
In the Graveyard at St Peter's Belton Uppingham

The Old Vicarage Belton, Uppingham

through to their conservatory and served me up a cool drink, and expressed his disappointment that Audrey was not home and therefore missing out on this opportunity to share her knowledge. He told me that he thought Charles Newmarch had written some other books, he thought were to do with travelling in the East but he wasn't sure.

I asked him about the vicarage, and he pointed me down the road to a B&B, which is now called "The Old Rectory", and thought that that may be the place. We chatted for a while before I took my leave, and Norman met us at the gate with a large envelope, fat with papers and a book of poetry written by him.

What amazing hospitality, that three total strangers, should take time out of their day, to chat, invite me in to their homes, serve me drinks, show me around the church, and share their knowledge so freely! I was so blessed again, and had gained a little insight into the life of a wonderful forefather and his family.

Moira's notes mention that 'The Belton Vicarage' was built in 1838-1839, "possibly on the site of an older house which was probably the Curate's house, 'Parsonage House'". It goes on to say that it had a barn and stables. I followed Phillip's directions and found 'The Old Rectory' only a short distance away. It was a huge rambling two storey gabled house, with stables and a barn, overlooking a garden and some treed areas. The proprietor kindly showed me through, and it was amazing to think that this may have been the place where Charles wrote "The Newmarch Pedigree", and lived and raised a family with Annie his wife.

It wasn't far to Rockingham Castle. The name 'Rockingham', is mentioned by Charles and George Newmarch in relation to their difficulties encountered in tracing the descendants of Thomas Newmarch.

They say that, *"Gascoigne, the antiquary, compiled some valuable papers on its (the family's) history, extending from the period of the Conquest down to his own time, and filling, it is stated, no less than seven chests: but these treasures unfortunately became the property of the second Earl of Strafford, who bequeathed them to Thomas Watson, (third son of Edward Lord Rockingham by his sister Anne), to whom he left his estates, and whose son and heir burnt every paper in the collection, in the fear that they might contain something, which if discovered, might prejudice his title."* (The Newmarch Pedigree page 35'36.) It is for this reason that The Newmarch Pedigree, doesn't go past about 1600AD in some branches the tree, including the only branch where the Newmarch name could have been carried down to the present day.

Rockingham Castle stood imposingly at the top of a long hill climb, and could be seen for quite a few miles around, while at the bottom of the hill, the thatched stone cottages of Rockingham village, with their pretty cottage gardens, sat comfortably lining the roadside. Unfortunately when I arrived, the castle had closed for the season, however it is interesting to note that, the owner of the castle is, James Saunders Watson, more than likely, a descendant of Thomas Watson mentioned above.

Chapter VIII

I still had time in the day to drive to Whatton in Nottinghamshire, which lay about 50 miles to the north of Rockingham. It appears that the Newmarch family has been connected with Whatton since the first Adam de Newmarch, grandson of Bernard de Newmarch (Neufmarche), married Adelina of Whatton, somewhere around A.D. 1100-1135, (The Newmarch Pedigree page 5).

I was very excited to be heading to Whatton, as The Newmarch Pedigree page 14, states: *"the Church of Whatton contains two monuments, one of them in alabaster, surmounted by the figure of a Knight clad in mail and rich armour, upon whose helmet appears the head and part of the body of a griffin compassed with a coronet.*

Below the figure are the Arms of Newmarch, five fussils in Fesse. On the sides of the monument are eighteen shields embossed, containing the arms, which the Knight in question was entitled to quarter. The monument bears the inscription of 'A*** Newmarch'".

The afternoon was cooling quickly as I walked with great anticipation towards the church porch through the churchyard, littered with colourful autumnal leaves.

The door was locked! No! This was such a dramatic piece of history. I spent twenty or thirty minutes looking for someone who may have a key. Then I phoned the numbers on the board – no answer. The notice board mentioned that the Vicar also had a church and congregation at Aslacton, (which was also mentioned in the family tree), and was nearby. I made the short drive to Aslacton but there was no response at the church or vicarage.

It seems that the Newmarches were Lords of the Manor of Whatton for several centuries. In the third year of the reign of Edward1, A.D. 1275, *"Henry de Newmarch is mentioned as having a charter of free fishing"*, (Page 19), which I thought about as I drove between Whatton and Aslacton, and passed over a body of water, (I think, The Devon River).

There is also mention of Thomas de Newmarch who was something of a warrior Knight, and *"in A.D. 1315, he was one of the Knights summoned to attend the King at Newcastle-Upon-Tyne, to repel the Scotch, in the eighth year of the reign of Edward 11"*. (Page 19′20). On a number of other occasions, he was appointed by the King to lead men into battle against the Scots.

In the twelfth year of the reign of Edward 111, (27/9/1338), *"a Charter of Market or Fair was granted to him in respect of his Manor of Whatton"*, Page 20. This Charter was apparently confirmed to his grandson Hugh de Newmarch in the first year of the reign of Richard 11, A.D. 1377. (Page 21).

I had a cup of tea at the pub, and was really praying for a way to get into the church as it was getting late, and I'd come a fair distance.

I returned once more to the church whose sign reads:
" *St John of Beverley, Whatton in the Vale"*.

To my absolute joy, there were two women attending a grave. The daughter had been visiting from abroad, and had come with her mother to attend to her late father's grave.

I told them of my predicament, and they made a quick phone call, and an elderly gentleman appeared within a few minutes, and kindly unlocked the huge gothic oak door. In my excitement, I almost fell down a step as my eye caught sight of the alabaster Knight on the opposite wall. It was so exciting, exactly as the text had said, except that Charles and George Newmarch believed that the Knight was Adam de Newmarch and there was a printed sign which read:

Sir Hugh Newmarch

Died about 1400 AD

Lord of the Manor of Whatton

The coat of arms with the shield and the "five fussils in fesse" were displayed in colour; The background of the shield was silver (Argent), the five fussils were like five vertically elongated diamonds in fesse (squashed together), gules (red). These according to Charles Newmarch are the Arms of Newmarch of Whatton, and the Arms of Newmarch of Bentley are, Gules (red shield), five fussils in fesse, (Or) (Gold). (The Newmarch Pedigree, page 18). Next to the Arms of Newmarch of Whatton on the sign were the Arms of Arden.

Unfortunately, part of Sir Hugh's, (or perhaps Adam de Newmarch's), left leg has been broken off. I did read an explanation for this somewhere. I believe it was something to do with striking a flint between his legs to light candles, and over time it fractured and knocked off his leg. Despite this, he was still resplendent in his chain mail.

The eighteen shields are there. Some of the coats of arms are worn and now difficult to see. It's hard to come to terms with the sense of history there. I would like to have lingered much longer, but after I'd taken some photos, I felt that I couldn't keep the kind gentleman waiting who had let me in, as he was hovering, so I thanked him immensely, and took my leave, so grateful to have had the opportunity to have gained entry.

Next to the church is a very large mansion, surrounded by very high old stone walls, named 'Whatton Grange', and I wondered if this could in fact have been the original Manor of Whatton, as it was substantial, and its lands seemed to go down to the river. Perhaps that is where the fishing rights were exercised?

This whole experience was so amazing, I was beginning to feel as if I was on an 'Indiana Jones' type treasure hunt, with The Newmarch Pedigree as my treasure map. I was also in awe of Charles and George Newmarch, who researched this document so accurately in 1868. The details are staggeringly accurate. Feeling flushed with success, I drove back to Launde Abbey, arriving just in time for a lovely dinner and some time with the patchwork ladies.

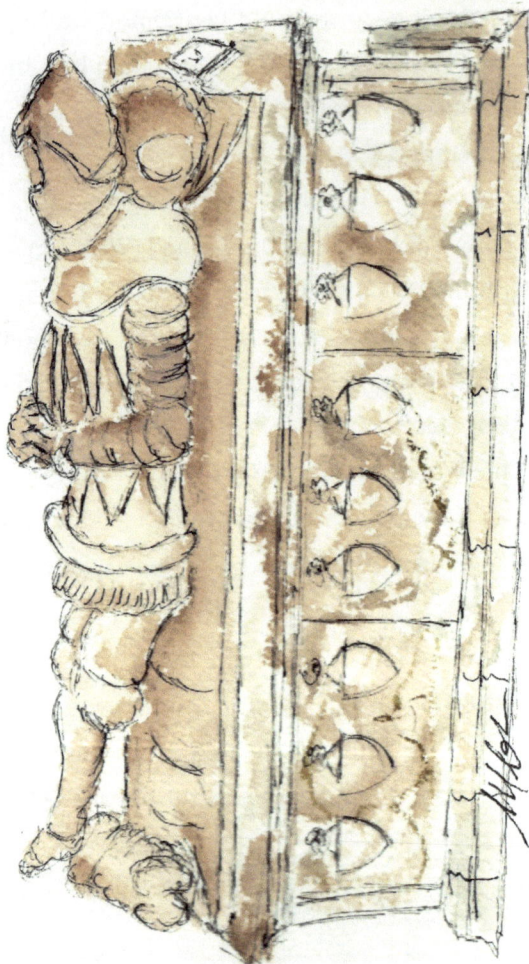

Alabaster Knight Effigy Circa 1400AD Sir Hugh de Newmarch or perhaps Sir Adam de

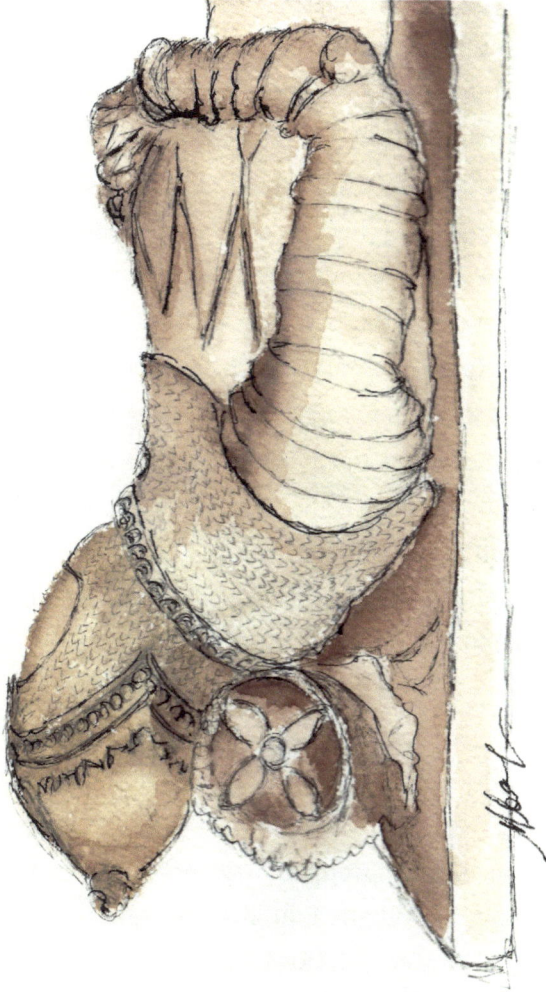

Close up of Sir Hugh (or Adam) showing Newmarch 'Five Fussils in Fesse' Coat of Arms on his Breastplate and Gauntlet

Chapter IX

I shared in the 7.00am Prayer Service in the main chapel, then following a good English breakfast of sausages and eggs, I farewelled Launde Abbey.

George (my GPS), led me through lovely country lanes to the A1 which I followed north to Lincolnshire where links to the Newmarch family can be traced at least as far back as A.D.1253, when Adam de Novo Mercato was granted a fair in his manor at Carleton Scroop, County Lincoln in the 37th year of the reign of Henry 111. (Gazetteer of Markets and Fairs to 1516: Index of Persons). This is the same Adam de Newmarch who was involved in the siege at Kenilworth as discussed in Chapter 6.

The quiet village of Rothwell, Lincolnshire settled comfortably amongst rolling hills, and the old church of St Mary Magdalene, with its square Norman tower, sat snuggly on the side of a hill, surrounded by sleepy fields. It is accessed up a rocky tree lined laneway. The church sign indicated that St Mary's was part of the Swallow Group of Churches

Edward Newmarch who was born on January, 1674, at Cabourne (just over the hill), married Alicia at Rothwell about 1700, and died in Rothwell Parish 10th May, 1723. William Newmarch their son was born there on 6th January, 1710. There is also a Joseph Newmarch born there 13th August, 1732, to Benjamin and Margaret. Surprisingly, the little church was open, so I was able to go in and contemplate the fact that Newmarch family members would have been sitting in these pews, more than 300 years ago. It was staggering! The little church and churchyard were neat and well cared for, and a sign on the Church Noticeboard advertised a Harvest Festival Service in the church the following Sunday,

" Refreshments after Service

Blacksmith's Arms".

I saw no one in Rothwell. A couple of cars were parked at The Blacksmith's Arms, and I passed a large holding, with substantial farm buildings, surrounded by high old stone walls, and I wondered if it had belonged to the family at some time.

Cabourne was equally deserted except for through traffic on the A46. St Nicholas Church sat on a bend on the high side of the road, in a shaded churchyard. The sign advertised: BCP Mattins, 3rd Sunday of the month. Many of the gravestones were old and the wording gone or illegible, so I was unable to see if they belonged to many of the generations of Newmarches who were born, married and died in this community, as far back as the 16th and 17th centuries. The church was locked so unfortunately I was unable to search for relics of our family history inside.

On the other side of the A46, opposite the church, there were significant old farm buildings, again behind high stone walls, and one wonders again if they have been or are Newmarch holdings.

A few miles to the north was Great Limber, also recorded as the home of some of the Newmarches from at least the 17th Century. It is substantially larger than

Rothwell and Cabourne, sporting a very cute general store and post office, quite a large pub, a community hall, school and a pretty lake in front of the church.

The Parish Church was accessed through an iconic lych-gate, and there was no problem with locked doors, as the ladies of the Parish were feverishly working to decorate the church for Harvest Festival and were expecting the entire school's children to arrive there in half an hour.

I was asked not to walk on the red carpet, which I considered to be hilarious, as they were about to be invaded by a whole school of children! I asked one of these busy workers if there was a toilet. The reply was, "No we don't have one, but just go out the back into the churchyard, there's no one about"! I had to, I was desperate, but it made me wonder what happened every Sunday!

There were some beautiful old buildings around, including an impressive thatched Tudor style house, well set back from the road in lovely gardens. I wondered if it may have been the Vicarage – the sign on the gate gave that indication: "Priest House".

A little further north was Thornton Curtis. A number of Newmarches are recorded as having been being born, married or buried there, again in the 16th and 17th centuries.

Its very interesting to travel to these places, which are simply place names in the genealogical index, but on visiting, it quickly becomes apparent how close they are to each other, and how people easily moved between them during their lives. At Thornton Curtis I had lunch at the 'Thornton Hunt Inn', and enjoyed their speciality, Lincoln Sausages, chips, and peas and gravy! From there I looked across to the historic 'Church of St. Lawrence', whose origins apparently date back to A.D. 1139, through an Augustinian Order of Canons who established an Abbey in the Parish.

I was fortunate to be able to go in, through the small open door in the huge oak door, as a Church Warden was taking a young lady architect in to inspect the tower. He invited me in to enjoy the church. I was struck by the black Tournai marble Baptismal font which dates to the 12th Century, and originated in what is now Belgium, and I wondered how many Newmarch babies had their heads wet from that font. Again, many Newmarches are recorded in the Births, Deaths and Marriages of Thornton Curtis, from at least 16th Century. It was beginning to rain as I walked out into the wet, leaf strewn churchyard, and drove the few miles to Barrow-upon-Humber, where there is also record of many Newmarches living there. I walked through the huge cemetery, but the elements have removed any trace of 16th and 17th Century names on headstones.

Driving into the village of Barton-upon-Humber, one can now look down on the mighty Humber River and the expansive Humber Bridge. The tide was low, revealing what looked like wide tidal mud flats. Travelling a few miles west, still on the south side of the Humber, the road climbed to South Ferriby, where more Newmarches had lived. I walked up to St. Nicholas Church, the rising path strewn with fallen ripe berries and apples from laden trees, which overhung the path. The view over the Humber was even more panoramic, but sadly this time I couldn't enter the locked church.

Stairway to Church Tower Great Limber Parish Church

Whirlow Grange Retreat House, in the leafy suburbs of Sheffield, was the site of my next two nights accommodation. Once a private home, it was built in the 1860's and is a gracious stone building set in manicured gardens. It has now been extended and adapted as a retreat/conference centre and is now a registered charity, which is run with the support of the Anglican Diocese of Sheffield.

The manager told me that I was the only guest in that night except for a Jewish group who had been fasting all week!

Chapter X

It was early Saturday morning as I enjoyed a delicious cooked breakfast in the ornate dining room, alone. The large picture windows revealed the garden, shrouded in misty rain. It was hard to believe that so much had happened in little more than a week since flying into Heathrow.

I drove northeast to Tickhill, in drizzly rain, arriving through an avenue of leafy mature trees. It appears that Ralph de Neufmarche, Bernard's son, *"had settled at Bentley-Cum-Arksey in Yorkshire, and to have been the companion of Roger de Busli, founder of the Honour of Tickhill in that County, of which honour Ralph and his descendants held four Knight's fees in Arksey. We find him to have been one of the witnesses to Roger de Busli's Charter, or grant of lands to the Priory of Blythe in Tickhill, Temp.2 W2,* (in the second year of the reign of King William 11), *A.D. 1088"*, Page 4 , The Newmarch Pedigree.

The literature shows that the 'Honour of Tickhill', refers to the substantial land holdings and manors, including Tickhill, which were granted to Roger de Busli. 'A Knight's fee' according to Wikipedia, was a sufficient amount of land from which a Knight could derive sustenance for himself and his esquires, and also to furnish them with horses and armour to fight for his overlord in battle. No money in rent was payable by the Knight, but he was expected to be available to fight for up to 40 days per year to defend his overlord. (Wikipedia on "Knight's Fee").

Candle Niche at St Lawrence's Church, Thornton Curtis

I passed very old stone high walls, with the name on the gate post, ' Friary Close ', and wondered if that could have been 'the priory' mentioned in the text. Next I passed by the castle before entering the busy medieval shopping street, and turning off to the church. It seemed that everyone in Tickhill was out, either trying to park their vehicle, or strolling happily down the street, pausing to greet friends and acquaintances.

I reversed into a space, where a young man was peering into the bonnet of his aged orange Ford Escort panel van. I apologized if I'd come too close, and he began to chat, along with his girlfriend who had left the passenger seat to join us. They asked me where I was from, and when I told them Australia, they shared with me their desire to live there.

I told them of my quest, and asked if they knew if 'Friary Close' was in fact the priory. They confirmed that it was, and asked me if I'd seen the castle yet. I mentioned that I'd passed it, and they went on to tell me that the local legend has it that there was a secret underground tunnel between the castle and the priory, which was built as an escape route for the monks, especially in the days of Cromwell, who set out to dismantle and destroy every monastery in Britain.

What an amazing piece of anecdotal information, which adds such colour and intrigue to the tale! Following a closer look at the castle and Friary Close, I left the quaint village of Tickhill and travelled further northeast to The Isle of Axholme, which is so called because that area of land once was the only high ground in a boggy marshland, which has

Tickhill Castle Gate

since been filled. The Isle of Axeholme is mentioned twice in our text, mostly in relation to the recorded history of the Isle of Axeholme: *"The figures of Ralph and Elizabeth his wife, as well as those of his four children, Robert, Hugh, Thomas and Elizabeth, whose names are given in 'Stonehouse's History of the Isle of Axeholme' were once to be seen in the windows of Wymersley Church".* Page 16, also Page 13.

I had no preconception of what I might find on the Isle of Axeholme, but happily for me, I came across the 'Old Rectory', which was the family home of the Wesleys', of Methodist Movement fame. It was the home in which Susannah Wesley bore 19 children, and only ten survived infancy. It was the home where John and Charles were raised, and miraculously survived a house fire, which was started by an angry mob of villagers who were at odds with Samuel Wesley, their father. I arrived just in time for an hour long guided tour of the property. This was such an unexpected bonus.

An old photo of the rectory shows many of the windows bricked up. This was because either, they were unable to afford the glass, as it was very expensive at that time, or it may have been because of the Daylight Tax, which was levied according to how many windows were in the house! Apparently this is how the expression "daylight robbery" came about. So if one was short of money, then the windows were permanently occluded to save paying the tax levied on that window. One wonders who conjured up such a diabolical law!

I drove on to nearby Althorp where *"Adam de Newmarch 4ᵗʰ married Elizabeth, daughter of Roger de Mowbray, with whom he received the lands in Althorp, Lincolnshire, which ultimately descended to Elizabeth de Newmarch who married John Nevill of Althorp, who built the church there in temp. Edward 1V, (1461-70), on the walls of which are the arms of Mowbray and Newmarch with those of Nevill are still extant".* (𝕿𝖍𝖊 𝕹𝖊𝖜𝖒𝖆𝖗𝖈𝖍 𝕻𝖊𝖉𝖎𝖌𝖗𝖊𝖊 𝕻𝖆𝖌𝖊 12).

It was a cold and wet Saturday afternoon, but the church was open with a sign welcoming visitors to the historic church. A few faithful ladies were there to help, including Joyce who was deaf but lip read excellently. She was the resident local history expert, and was a mine of information. First things first – the ladies made me a cup of tea, then I was shown the Newmarch/Neville Coat of arms on the church wall. The Neville Coat of Arms is like a blue St. Andrews Cross, and the Newmarch five fussils in fesse, were adjacent. The coat of arms was in plaster relief, and surrounded by floral motif.

Joyce told me that the original church was built on land given by Roger de Mowbray and was probably built by him.

Sir John Neville built the current church, in 1483, and was the 9ᵗʰ great grandson-in-law of Roger de Mowbray. The arms of Mowbray, Newmarch and Neville are quartered together on the church tower outside. The Mowbray Arms displayed is 'the lion rampant'. 𝕿𝖍𝖊 𝕹𝖊𝖜𝖒𝖆𝖗𝖈𝖍 𝕻𝖊𝖉𝖎𝖌𝖗𝖊𝖊, 𝕻𝖆𝖌𝖊 25 confirms this: *"In right of his wife, Sir John Nevill became possessed of Wymersley, Scothorp, and Askrigg in Co. York,*

Whatton and other manors in Co. Notts, and Althorp in Co. Lincoln, at which latter place he built the church, completed circa 1483, upon the tower of which the arms of Nevill and those of Newmarch, with Mowbray quartered, still appear."

Yes, amazingly all these years later they are still visible.

Arms of Neville and Newmarch in Althorp Church

Joyce had some official looking historical documentation for the Nevilles, which showed that John Neville's parents were Sir Ralph de Neville, Earl of Westmoreland, and Mary de Ferrers, Lady of Oversley.

Their son John Neville Esq., who was born in 1416, was Sheriff of Lincolnshire, and Married Elizabeth Newmarch, the daughter of Robert and Joanna Newmarch.

Their daughter Margaret Neville, (born 1441), married Thomas Wentworth, and their other daughter Jane (Joane) Neville, married Sir William Gascoigne. (This information will become more relevant in due course).

The Lid of the Baptismal Font in St Oseald's Althorp

𝕿𝖍𝖊 𝕹𝖊𝖜𝖒𝖆𝖗𝖈𝖍 𝕻𝖊𝖉𝖎𝖌𝖗𝖊𝖊 only agrees with these assertions in part. Firstly our text, 𝕻𝖆𝖌𝖊 24, asserts that Joanna Nevill was the only issue of Elizabeth de Newmarch and John Nevill, and agrees that she married Sir William Gascoigne.

It was then a further four generations on, before Margaret Gascoigne, the daughter of Sir William Gascoigne 1V, married Thomas Wentworth of Wentworth Woodhouse in about 1560, which would have made Margaret Neville (born 1441), 119 years old at the time! There was a Margaret Nevill who was the daughter of Richard Neville, (Lord Latimer), and she was the second wife of Sir William Gascoigne 11.

I showed Joyce the family tree in the back of 𝕿𝖍𝖊 𝕹𝖊𝖜𝖒𝖆𝖗𝖈𝖍 𝕻𝖊𝖉𝖎𝖌𝖗𝖊𝖊. Her response was, " It reads like the Who's Who of British Aristocracy"! I was pleased to be able to share it with her, given her keen interest in the local history.

One of the posters on the wall refers to the church's close links with 'The Knights Templar', saying that Roger de Mowbray, who was himself an earnest Crusader in the 12th Century, had given the Knights Templar lands on which they built a preceptory, and hospital.

One of the ladies actually went home to bring back a copy of "History of St Oswald's" for me, when none could be found after a thorough search in the church.

What an interesting visit that was. I took some photos of the arms on the tower and waved goodbye to Joyce, who lived next door.

Symbol of the Knights Templar-The Knights of St John

95

Althorp is on the Trent River, not far from where it flows into the Humber. The Newmarch Pedigree Page 12 states: *"The Rotuli Hundredorum record his* (Adam de Newmarch), *possession of a weir, with rights of fishing, in the Trent at Althorp, and jurisdiction over felons at Carleton, there called 'Karleton' 4 Edward1* (1276). I wondered whether in this instance 'felons' were poachers? Very curious!

The afternoon was dull and misty as I made my way through Winterton to Winteringham which is probably only 20 miles or so north of the Isle of Axeholme, which I mentioned earlier in the chapter in relation to the recorded history of the Isle of Axeholme: *"The figures of Ralph and Elizabeth his wife, as well as those of his four children, Robert, Hugh, Thomas and Elizabeth, whose names are given in 'Stonehouse's History of the Isle of Axeholme'".* Page 16, also Page 13.

Charles Newmarch explains that this marriage of Ralph and Elizabeth is significant, as Elizabeth is the heiress of Hugh de Newmarch, Lord of the Manor of Whatton, whose alabaster effigy I visited in the Church at Whatton and discussed earlier.

Ralph, the son of Robert de Newmarch is from the Bentley/ Wymersley line, which includes, the Adam who was involved in the Seige of Kenilworth. Ralph himself was a Knight, *"and was engaged in the Battle of Shewsbury in 4 Henry 1V, A.D. 1403, and was there slain".* (The Newmarch Pedigree Page 16). Thus the marriage brought the two family lines together. Of their four children, Hugh died without issue and it is thought that he died quite young, Robert and his wife Joanna had only one daughter Elizabeth, who married John Neville of Althorp, and so through his line came the Nevilles, Gascoignes and Wentworths. Elizabeth appears not to have married, so it is through Thomas that all future generations bearing the Newmarch name must come.

"This branch of the family, then, we find settled at Winteringham, a parish lying on the southern bank of the Humber at the northern extremity of the County of Lincoln, and not very far from Althorp, one of the seats of the old family.

Sir Robert Newmarch (son of Thomas), was living there in 1481, but after that our record of him ceases", (The Newmarch Pedigree, Page 35), and in Page 36, "The earliest register of the Parish of Winteringham contains an entry of the burial of John Newmarch, on the 17th December, 1599".

Winteringham sits on a rise – almost like a levy bank, several hundred metres from the banks of the Humber. The houses are very old for the most part, some with high walls made of river stones and hand made bricks. I noticed one stone house bearing the plaque "WALNUT 1670", which was just one of the many very old buildings which had been restored and proudly wore its history. There were sizeable historic stone and brick barns and farm buildings, and an old coach house, some of which have now been converted for residential use.

On that wet Saturday afternoon, the historic village exuded peace and contentment, however 'The Bay Horse Inn' was abuzz, and I wondered if the whole village was in there!

I drove down across the lower river flats to Winteringham Haven and through the drizzle could see the masts of the locals' yachts on their moorings, and one on the slips.

I headed back up into the village, and turned east along the high road to follow the Humber, and came to 'Winteringham Grange', a farm with substantial historic buildings. Again, there is the perpetual question, was this a Newmarch property?

I soon arrived at the South Ferriby Lock, which was the gatekeeper between the South Channel of the Humber and the New Ancholme/Weir Dike, where tied up, there were river barges, the carriers of freight to the heart of Lincolnshire.

In a few short miles, I reached the Humber Bridge, and crossed the wide expanse of river to Hessle, whose earliest records have entries of births, deaths and marriages of Newmarches from 1568, (Page 37).

The Parish Church of All Saints, Hessle, was open and illuminated, and quite a crowd filled the pews, as an orchestral concert was about to begin. The lady on the door, assuming I was coming to the concert, tried to sell me a ticket. I explained I wasn't there for the concert, and after a quick scan of the interior from the entrance, I took my leave and pushed on through Kingston-Upon-Hull to Hedon, a medieval market town, where a number of descendants of George Newmarch lived in the 17th century.

The narrow winding streets and interesting two and three storey buildings fronting the street, and the Market Square, gave it a air of community, similar to that of Tickhill.

'Walnut' C1670 in Winteringham

The Queen's Head pub, and other buildings were Tudor style gabled buildings, white with blackened beams and woodwork. There were old, hand made brick buildings, and others were Georgian style painted cream or white.

The church of St Augustine was closed, and the afternoon was almost gone, so I set the GPS for Sheffield and headed back through the rain. After a lovely roast dinner at 'Toby Carvery', I sat in the sitting room at Whirlow, writing my diary, as the very chatty Jewish group debated 'the God Question', to use their phrase.

Chapter XI

Wentworth Woodhouse was my next destination, just a short 10 or 12 mile drive north east of Sheffield. Already mentioned, is the line of descent from the Newmarches through the Nevilles and Gascoignes to the Wentworths, and here note The Newmarch Pedigree Page 24, 2; "*Margaret Gascoigne married Thomas Wentworth, of Wentworth Woodhouse, Co. York, by which union the titles and estates of the families of Newmarch, Ferrers of Oversley, and Nevill of Raby, devolved upon the Wentworths, and were subsequently recognized in the Patent, by which Thomas Wentworth was elevated to the peerage, to be hereafter noticed. By this marriage, there was one son William and four daughters*".

The road sign "Wentworth", announced my arrival, and I was immediately aware of seemingly endless high stonewalls on both sides of the road. Another sign at the T intersection, directed me to 'Wentworth Woodhouse', which until recently has been the seat of power of the Wentworths, and later, the Earls Fitzwilliam through inheritance since the 16th century.

The first point of public access to 'Wentworth Woodhouse' was to the retail nursery car park, which, being Sunday, had become a 'Farmers Market'. As it was still quite early, and a little drizzly, there were not too many people about at that time. I walked down through the extensive nursery area to the tearoom, in an attempt to gain a glimpse of the famous 'house', but unfortunately it was closed for a private function.

Disappointed, I walked through rows of statues of cherubim, birdbaths and fountains and strained to get a peek of the estate through the closed high gates at the end of the yard, with little success. Happily for me though, I struck up a conversation with a local couple, who told me that it was possible to see the house from the Public Footpath, which ran right past the house! They told me I should look for a book called "Black Diamonds", which talks about some of the history of Wentworth Woodhouse.

Buoyed by this information, I retraced my steps and perused the lovely fresh and colourful produce at the Farmers' Market, where succulent red strawberries and tomatoes, contrasted with rich green cucumbers and capsicums, and the plump vibrant oranges and pumpkins, with fat purple 'red' onions. Baskets of fresh laid brown and white hens eggs begged to be taken home and enjoyed.

Past the nursery was the entrance to the Wentworth Woodhouse Home Farm, where there were extensive, very large stone farm buildings and stables. I peeked in through one of the many arches in a very long building, and frightened a pen of little porkers, who all squealed loudly in protest as I took their photo.

A couple of hundred metres further on, outside the high stonewall, was a parking layby, where I left the car and walked through a gateway, where a sign read,

"Fitzwilliam/Wentworth Estates
        PRIVATE ROAD
PUBLIC FOOTPATH ONLY

No Cycling

Dogs to be kept on lead at all times".

Through the avenue of trees, one could see a stone cottage over to the right; I guessed it was more than likely the gatekeeper's cottage. I continued under the canopy of trees, passing dog walkers and joggers, in the short distance to open ground, grassed and expansive. Then, over to my right, was what I believed to be Wentworth Woodhouse, the longest house in Europe at 606ft, (reportedly, twice the size of Buckingham Palace), which boasts 365 rooms and is set amongst 150 acres of park and gardens, and 90,000 acres. It looked enormous, but I realized later that this was only the side view! Amazingly I later discovered that this was not the house, but merely the Stable Block, which makes it even more amazing and audacious!

However, the imposing brown stone building stood forlorn and drab, and showed signs of neglect, a reflection of its chequered history perhaps, which is full of intrigue and innuendo.

At the beginning of the chapter, I noted that the only son of Sir Thomas Wentworth and Margaret Gascoigne, was Sir William Wentworth, who was born in 1562, and married Anne Atkinson. They had 10 children, eight boys and two girls. According to our text (Page 26), the eldest son John died young, so Thomas, the second son, born 13th April, 1593, succeeded to his father's title and estates on his coming of age in 1614. He entered Parliament in 1621 during the reign of James 1, and sat in the House of Commons into the reign of Charles 1.

The Stable Block at 'Wentworth Woodhouse' from the Public Path

He gained favour with the King, who on 22nd July, 1628, elevated him to the peerage with the title, *"Baron Wentworth of Wentworth Woodhouse, Newmarch, and Oversley"*, and created him, *"Viscount Wentworth"* in the same year.

The following January, he was constituted *"President of the Council of the North, Lord Lieutenant of the County of York, and a Member of the Privy Council"*. In 1632, he was appointed *"Lord Deputy of Ireland"* and by his 'able and judicious administration of that government's affairs was instrumental in restoring order and prosperity'.

He was sent for by the King to assist with affairs at home, and shortly afterwards was created, *'Earl of Strafford'* and *'Baron Raby, of Raby, Co. Durham'*. This Barony was *"specially limited, in event of failure of his own male issue, to his brothers and their issue male"*, (The Newmarch Pedigree, Page 27).

One can imagine, that *"being the most trusted of the King's advisors"*, and having so many favours bestowed on him by the King, earned for himself many jealous enemies at Court, to the point, that his enemies conspired to have him impeached for high treason, falsely accusing him without cause. They moved swiftly, and without even awaiting his defence, effected their purpose by 'Bill of Attainder', while the trial was still pending. (The Newmarch Pedigree, Page 29).

This had desperate consequences. Wikipedia states that under English Common Law, the criminal who was charged under this Bill, was 'tainted', or 'attained', and lost all civil rights including a fair trial, as well as that, any owned property was forfeited to the Crown, and could no longer be passed to the family by will or testament, and any peerage titles would also revert to the Crown!

Sadly for Thomas Wentworth, King Charles 1 failed to come to his aid, and he was beheaded on Tower Hill on 12th May, 1641. The Newmarch Pedigree, Page 31, quotes Kennett,

"Fell this noble Earl, who, if his master could have saved him, might have saved his master; this was indeed, the blow that by degrees reached up to the King's own head", thus alluding to the subsequent execution of the king.

The text goes on to reveal, that Thomas was married three times, and had a son, William, by his second wife, the daughter of the Earl of Clare.

This William Wentworth *"had all his father's honours, formally conferred on him, by an Act passed in the 14th year of the reign of Charles 11, (1662), by which his father's attainder was reversed".* Having lost his head, this was a little late to be of comfort for Thomas, Earl of Strafford!

Unfortunately, his son, Sir William, 2nd Earl of Strafford, now heir to the restored fortunes and titles of his father, died without issue, and as already mentioned in this case, the Barony of Raby could only be passed to the brothers or their male issue of the first Baron of Raby, (the first Earl of Strafford).

One of Sir Thomas's brothers was William, whose son Thomas, the grandson of the 1st Sir William Wentworth, rightly inherited the Barony of Raby, however, he somehow was cheated out of inheriting Wentworth Woodhouse, when it was passed to Thomas Watson, the nephew of Sir William, the 2nd Earl of Strafford's <u>wife</u>, who not being a direct male descendant, could not inherit the Barony of Raby!

This is the very same Thomas Watson who was referred to in 𝕮𝖍𝖆𝖕𝖙𝖊𝖗 7 of the text, in relation to Rockingham Castle, and the very same Thomas Watson, who burned the seven chests of manuscripts of family history, compiled in the 17th century by Richard Gascoigne! This act, according to Wikipedia, (which corroborates assertions made in 𝕿𝖍𝖊 𝕹𝖊𝖜𝖒𝖆𝖗𝖈𝖍 𝕻𝖊𝖉𝖎𝖌𝖗𝖊𝖊), occurred at the time when he was created Earl of Malton in 1728, and was reportedly done on the advice of his attorney, in case there was incriminating evidence which would prejudice his title!

To rub salt into the wound for Thomas Wentworth, Watson had added 'Wentworth' to his name, from then on was known as Thomas Watson-Wentworth! The arrogance seems breathtaking!

He was a Member of Parliament and in 1733, was made 'Baron Harrowden, Baron Wrath, Viscount Higham, and Earl of Malton'. He inherited the Barony of Rockingham from his first cousin once removed. Two months after succeeding in the Barony of Rockingham, he was created 'Marquess of Rockingham' in 1746.

At Wentworth Woodhouse, he entirely rebuilt an existing Jacobean house, which had been the home of the first Sir Thomas Wentworth. Thomas Watson-Wentworth and his son and heir Charles Watson-Wentworth, (2nd Marquess of Rockingham), who became Prime Minister twice, expanded the house even further, making it an important Whig powerhouse, (Wikipedia).

Eventually, Wentworth Woodhouse, with all its contents, passed to the family of the 2nd Marquess' sister, the Earls Fitzwilliam. This was the beginning of a dynasty, which lasted into the second half of the 20th century.

The Fitzwilliams were coal barons, earning millions of pounds from rich coal seams on their land. Unlike other coal mine owners in the 19th and early 20th centuries, the Fitzwilliams were good to their employees and respected by them. The village of Wentworth was a coal mining village, where men and boys left their homes every morning to 'go down the pit', for meager wages.

There were plenty of family feuds through the years in the Fitzwilliam mansion over inheritance, and the scandal of Lord Fitzwilliam V1's eldest son, William, Viscount Milton, who was diagnosed with mental illness, and sent away to an 'asylum for the insane' because he had epilepsy! ("Black Diamonds", p. 27, Catherine Bailley).

Following in the footsteps of Thomas Watson-Wentworth, the Fitzwilliams were obsessive in removing all traces of their past, and according to Catherine Bailley, in her book "Black Diamonds", which catalogues the rise and fall in the fortunes of the Fitzwilliams, she tells of a bonfire when sixteen tons of family documents were heaped and burnt, in a fire that lasted for three weeks, (Page xxii). This was not unusual for the family, as after the death each of the 7th, 8th and 9th Earls, their private papers were burnt in a bid to hide their past.

In an act of class jealousy, the 99 acres of lawns and woods and gardens of Wentworth Woodhouse were mined in

1946, by order of Manny Shinnwell, the Labour Party
Minister for Fuel and Power, on the pretext of the desperate
need for fuel in post war Britain. It was however an act of
wanton destruction and left 50ft high piles of rubble and
ancient uprooted trees, in front of the family's windows,
(Wikipedia).

The Nationalization of Coal Mines, and skyrocketing
Death Duties severely reduced the family's wealth, and
perhaps some squandering and mismanagement of the
family fortune, left the family no choice but to find ways to
save the house. According to Wikipedia, in the 1940's, The
Ministry of Health tried to requisition the house as housing
for homeless industrial families.

In 1949, Lady Mabel Fitzwiliam, was able to negotiate a
deal, where most of the house was leased out as an
educational establishment, leaving a 40 room apartment for
the use of the family. This continued in various forms until
1988.

Wentworth Woodhouse was subsequently sold, and is
now privately owned again and undergoing renovation.

Staggered by the size of the estate, I headed into the
village of Wentworth and went to the 'Church of Old Holy
Trinity', which stood under tall oaks on a hillside below the
newer parish church. The Old Church was a little
dilapidated, and partly unroofed in one section, and it was
surrounded by the tombstones of generations.

On that damp morning, it was manned by enthusiastic
and knowledgeable members of The Churches Conservation
Trust, (www.visitchurches.org.uk), which is the English

national charity protecting historic churches at risk. They explained in detail many of the monuments and plaques, which adorned the stone sanctuary that dated back to 1491, although there is record of a church on that site from 1235. According to the information leaflet, this was the church in which John Wesley preached in 1733.

The 𝔑ewmarch 𝔓ebigree, 𝔓age 31, in discussing William Wentworth, 2nd Earl of Strafford, states that, *"he erected a monument in the Church of Wentworth Woodhouse to the memory of his father, and another for himself, on which later, his name and titles were thus inscribed: "William Wentworth, Earl of Strafford, Viscount Wentworth, Baron Wentworth of Wentworth Woodhouse, Newmarch, Oversley, and Raby"*.

This inscription on brass plates, is only part of the long and detailed discourse about his family, and particularly his wife, Henrietta Maria Stanley whom William speaks about in glowing terms, such that, "never did a wife more passionately love her husband".

The two brass plates are set towards the base of an elaborate, ornately carved stone monument, which is mounted on the church wall, and depicts William and Henrietta kneeling in prayer, facing one another, beneath stone drapes, drawn back on each side to reveal the couple.

The memorial to Sir Thomas 1st Earl of Strafford, as mentioned above, which was erected by his son, William, lists all the 1st Earl of Strafford's titles which were listed earlier, including *'Baron of Wentworth Woodhouse, Newmarch'*, etc. It is not unlike the memorial to William and

Henrietta, but in this case, The Earl of Strafford is kneeling and praying alone.

The oldest memorial in the church, is a brass plate set into the floor, and dates from 1548, and commemorates the 1st Thomas Wentworth.

In the church, there is a large 'Chest Tomb', dating from 1587, apparently containing the remains of Thomas Wentworth and Margaret Gascoigne. Stone effigies of the couple rest on top of the chest.

There was an eye catching monument in coloured marble, wall mounted and showing in relief, the entire family of Sir William Wentworth (son of Margaret Gascoigne, and Sir Thomas Wentworth), and his wife Anne. The parents are facing each other, praying, and below are seven of the sons, on the left. In the centre is their famous brother 1st Earl of Strafford, and to the right there are three girls facing towards the centre. This is curious, as our text records only two girls.

One other feature of the church was the Fitzwilliam Crypt, which I descended to via a stone, slightly mossy staircase. It was dark and damp down there, and was the resting place of many Fitzwilliams, including Viscount Milton, (the epileptic), and his wife, Laura.

Ian, on duty for The Churches Conservation Trust, told me about 'The Wentworth Papers', which were still available to purchase through some booksellers, and contained valuable information about the family history. I thanked him for the amazing visit, and made my way to Wentworth Castle.

Decorative Marble Memorial of the First Sir William Wentworth

Showing the First Earl of Strafford Kneeling Alone

Chapter XII

A mere six miles from Wentworth Woodhouse, was Wentworth Castle, which was once known as 'Stainborough Castle', and was purchased in 1708 by Thomas Wentworth, Lord Raby, and grandson of Sir William Wentworth.

Embittered by the passing of the Wentworth fortune, (including Wentworth Woodhouse), which he believed to be his birthright, to Thomas Watson, Thomas Wentworth set out to rival and surpass Watson by making the Wentworth Castle estate, more splendid than Wentworth Woodhouse, from the architecture of the buildings and the artworks contained in them, to the parks and gardens.

The Newmarch Pedigree, Page 32 states that Thomas Wentworth, Baron of Raby: *"greatly distinguished himself in the Campaigns in Flanders, and as Ambassador extraordinary to the States General in the reign of Queen Anne, for which services, as well as in remembrance of his great uncle, he was created Earl of Strafford and Viscount Wentworth, by patent dated 4th September, 1711"*.

Thomas Newmarch's time in Europe, and the elevation of his status and fortune, gave him access to European architects, who drew designs for the rebuilding of the grandiose house as well as artworks for the collection, which he would house in a gallery one hundred and eighty feet long, twenty-four feet wide, and thirty feet high, (Wikipedia on 'Wentworth Castle').

The majestic avenue of oak trees, which was the driveway, snaked its way up through lush pastures, where deer could be glimpsed feeding on the open grasslands.

Emerging through the trees, Wentworth castle stood in all its glory, not in the form of a medieval castle, as one may imagine a castle with turrets and towers, but in the form of a gracious Georgian three storey manor house. From its position, on a grassy clearing on the hillside, it commanded panoramic vistas of the estate, and indeed the surrounding countryside.

Following a quick bite of lunch in the café, I paid my entry fee, which did not give entry to the mansion, but only to the extensive gardens and 'Stainborough Castle', which is now the name for the sham castle at the top of the garden.

I was however able to access St James Chapel where caterers were setting up for a wedding. To my amazement, as I looked up to the gallery, the central panel of three old oak panels, below the gallery rail, bore the family coat of arms. Twelve coats of arms were represented, by 'quartering', including Mowbray, Neville, and NEWMARCH: five fussils in fesse in gold, on red background! I felt that this had made the visit very worthwhile, and was an unexpected find.

With a spring in my step, I made my way to the top of the hill through elaborate formal gardens, sculptures and monuments, and extensive plantings and avenues of trees, apparently the work of Thomas Wentworth. There at the top were the ruins of what one would consider to be a real castle, built originally with four towers, one for each of his four children, now only two remain. Built by Thomas Wentworth in 1726 as a sham castle to enhance the garden, and to be seen by all around as a token of his standing and I would imagine, to be seen and envied, by Thomas Watson.

In the bookshop afterwards, I was delighted to be able to purchase a copy of 'Black Diamonds', by Catherine Bailley, which had been recommended to me as an historical work about Wentworth Woodhouse, and the families who lived there.

It was time to move on to Bentley, which is mentioned in the text, Page 4, and states that Ralph de Newmarch, probably accompanied his father, Bernard de Newmarch, at the Battle of Hastings, and *"seems to have settled in Bentley-cum-Arksey"*. As previously discussed, he was the companion of Roger de Busli, founder of the Honour of Tickhill, and he and his descendants, *"held four knights fees in Arksey"*.

Bentley looked a little run down and degraded. The church was locked, and as I found nothing, which appeared to reveal any secrets from the past, I continued the short distance to Arksey, where there were some very old buildings, one with a courtyard, accessed by a high stone archway, which may have been a priory perhaps. There were other very interesting old buildings, but without local knowledge, one could only wonder at their history.

A little further down the road was Barnby Dun, formerly known as Barnby-upon-Don, which along with Bolton and Wymersley, were among Ralph de Newmarch's

Coat of Arms in St James' Chapel showing the Newmarch Five Fussils in Fesse Quartered on the shield

Part of the Garden Folly at Wentworth Castle

Beautiful Avenue of trees at Wentworth Castle

possessions, (Page 4). Also, *"the Newmarches presented to the rectory at Barnby-upon-Don from the earliest period to which the See of York extend down to the reign of Edward 111. (1327-1377).*

The Arms preserved in the chancel window of Barnby Church, serve to identify the family, (Page 5).

I was fortunate to find a lady who had keys to open The Parish Church of St Peter & St Paul, Barnby Dun. I was unable to find the Arms on the chancel window, as described on Page 5. A brochure in the church, detailing the history of the church stated that the chancel had to be entirely rebuilt, due to neglect by successive lay rectors. This refurbishment was completed in 1862, which reasonably explains why Charles Newmarch mentioned the chancel window, as his source was "Stonehouse's Isle of Axholme", which was published in 1839, when the Newmarch Arms were still present.

I did however have one find! On an oak board, with gold lettering, which listed "incumbents", and vicars, I discovered "Thomas de Newmarch", listed as an incumbent in 1299. He was only fourth in the list, which began with, 'Benedict', in 1244! It was obviously only for a short time, as "Henry de Deschington", was listed below Thomas, also at 1299.

The board then notes, that the Parish became a 'Vicarage', in 1343, following the appropriation of the 'Rectory' to the Collegiate Church of Cotterstock, Northants.

There are further references to this area in reference to Adam de Novo Mercato of 'Seige of Kenilworth' fame, who we discussed in chapter six, as having his manors in Bentley, Wymersley, Campsall and Thorne, Thorpe-in Balne, and all his lands in the county of Lincoln, seized under the King's warrant.

As a result of the 'Dictum of Kenilworth', there was restitution of these estates, but with conditions which, *"deprived his son in favour of his daughter and her issue, which were afterwards carried into effect",* (The Newmarch Pedigree, Page 10-11).

According to the text, Page 11, "inquisitions" or surveys were taken in the third and fourth years of the reign of Edward 1 (1275-1276), *"in pursuance of the commission issued under the great seal for ascertaining the demesnes of the crown, and to enquire of knight's fees, escheats, wardships, encroachments, and the like, and contained under the rolls known as 'Rotuli Hundredorum'. It records Adam de Novo Mercato in possession of Bentley and Arkseye, and as holding a knight's fee in Carleton, Co. Lincoln..... His widow's name was Joan, as appears not only from the Harleian M.S.S., but from the rolls of parliament, which record her claim for dower out of lands at Bentley 18 Edward 1, A.D.1290, and also from the records of the See of York, which contains her presentment of a clerk to the rectory of Barnby-upon-Don in 1299".* One wonders if there is any connection with Thomas de Newmarch being listed as the 'incumbent' in 1299 in the church at Barnby Dun, as observed above?

I believe that these 'inquisitions' were primarily to tally up who owned what, and to determine where taxes could be levied, but in understanding the above paragraph, perhaps some definitions would be in order:

'Demesne of the Crown' began with the Norman Conquest, when the King claimed all the land in England as his own. He then made grants of large parcels of land, mostly as feudal baronies, and the remaining land was part of the 'demesne of the Crown', and contained royal manors and hunting forests, which were leased to the sheriff of that shire. The annual fee for these, gave revenue to fund the royal administration. Forfeited lands also became part of the 'demesne of the crown'. (Wikipaedia on 'Demesne').

'Escheat' refers to the reversion of property to the Crown, where a person dies without a legal heir, (Wikipaedia on Escheats).

'Wardships' from the Act 1267, refer to the holding of lands, when the heir is a minor, until he/she, reaches full age. (Wikipaedia on 'Wardships').

The text goes on to put the death of this Adam at A.D. 1276, and that his son Adam had his father's lands at Carleton, and that about that time or soon after, *"Bentley and some of the larger fees passed into the hands of the Tibetots. This alienation was affected through Eva de Newmarch, daughter of Adam, who was married to Robert Tibetot".* (Page 12).

Adam's descendants did however retain *"Wymersley, Warmsworth, and some other manors, probably under the arrangements to which we have referred, by which provision was made for the heir of the great baron, whose repeated acts of rebellion had led to an enforced alienation of his larger fees"*, (page 12).

I next visited Thorpe-in-Balne and Thorne, both found in low-lying marshlands, where I passed the pot-like towers of the disused Thorpe Marsh Power Station. The six cooling towers are all that remain, each towering 340 feet into the air, and having an enormous girth at the base of 260 feet. Both Thorpe-in Balne and Thorne are mentioned in the text, as locations of manors held by the Newmarches from the 12th and 13th centuries. Whilst I saw some very old impressive buildings, I had no way of knowing if these had been Newmarch holdings.

Very satisfied by yet another full and amazing day, I made my way north, to the walled city of York, arriving just before dark at 'The Bar Convent'.

Chapter XIII

The city of York has since Roman times, been protected by city walls with entry points through gatehouses called 'Bars'. There are four main bars: Bootham Bar, Monk Bar, Walmgate Bar, and Micklegate Bar. There are also two smaller bars: Fishergate Bar, and Victoria Bar.

Each of these bars is like a small fortress in itself, having three or four storeys, and Walmgate Bar actually has its very own barbican, which is a separate, though very elaborate building which is built outside the city wall, but is connected by some type of walkway to the entry point.

The Bar Convent was situated just outside Mickelgate Bar, and is the oldest living convent in England, having been founded by Frances Bedingfield in 1686, at a time when Catholics were being persecuted. At that time it was a secret community, and was known as, "Ladies at the Bar", where they set up and ran boarding and day schools for Catholic girls. For this reason, the chapel is not obvious from the street, and its existence is hidden within the four storey, Georgian brick façade, which is right on the footpath. The circular chapel, is located on the top floor, and boasts a beautiful dome roof, and in case of a raid, eight exits, and a priest hole!

I parked in the paid council car park across Nunnery Lane, and rang the bell on the impressive entry door in the long, handsome building. Sister Mary, an elderly smiling lady dressed in a woollen skirt and cardigan, greeted me warmly. She led me upstairs to my room on the first floor, which was small but

Micklegate Bar

welcoming, and sported a small, hand painted disc on the door, labelling the room, "St James". She then took me for a tour through the convent, up and down stairs, pointing out the library, two TV rooms, the laundry, and the beautiful domed chapel, and then the private quarters of the Sisters, which were out of bounds.

My bedroom window overlooked the lovely mosaic tiled courtyard downstairs, which was enclosed under a high pitched glass roof, and served as a spacious entry hall, and overflow for the café/ guest breakfast room.

As I left the Convent in search of some dinner, Micklegate Bar was illuminated and looked majestic, standing four storeys high, its two turretted towers, were highlighted against the night sky by spotlights. Since 1389, Micklegate Bar has been, and still is the traditional, ceremonial gate for monarchs to enter the city of York.

Next morning, following a good sleep, I awoke to rain, and after a great cooked breakfast in the café downstairs, I headed off on foot, taking much pleasure in entering 'the city' through the wide stone archway of Mickelgate Bar.

My visit to York was not to search out Newmarches from The Newmarch Pedigree, even though some were alive before the text was written in 1868. As Charles Newmarch was unable to continue the trail of the family, following the burning of the seven chests of documents by Thomas Watson, as noted earlier, I began tracking backwards from my great grandfather, Alfred Newmarch.

Alfred Newmarch sailed into Sydney Harbour on the HMS Parramatta, from England, on Christmas Day, 1885, at just eighteen years of age, unaccompanied, as an 'unassisted immigrant'. To my astonishment through 'Googling', 'Alfred Newmarch, Accountant', I found an article from the Sydney Morning Herald in 1940, in which I read that he was a son of Colonel Henry Fowler Newmarch of the Bengal Staff Corps, India! I subsequently learned that he was born in India in 1867, and that his mother was, Marianne Eliza Julianna Davies.

MR. ALFRED NEWMARCH.

Mr. Alfred Newmarch, a city chartered accountant, died at his residence, High Street, Manly, last Wednesday. Mr. Newmarch was a son of the late Colonel Henry Fowler Newmarch, of the Bombay Staff Corps. For many years he held the position of accountant in the Master in Equity's Department, Sydney. He resigned to practise on his own account, and afterwards as Alfred Newmarch and Allison, and subsequently as Alfred Newmarch and Rockwell.

Mr. Newmarch married Harriet, daughter of Mrs. Catherine Robinson, of Croydon, who predeceased him. He is survived by three daughters.

The Sydney Morning Herald newspaper article from 12th June, 1940 Page 18 (National Library of Australia)

There was no doubt that this Alfred Newmarch was in fact my great grandfather, as "his residence at High Street, Manly", was my childhood home, and also of my father Colin Alfred Chapman, then known as 6 High Street, but now I believe, 2 High Street.

It was originally, Alfred and family's seaside holiday home, as they lived in a sizeable mansion in Grosvenor Road Turramurra, known as 'Maltorendi'.

The story goes, that during the Great Depression of the 1920's, Alfred's business partner misappropriated the Trust Funds which were held by the company. Alfred, being an honorable Christian man, sold the family mansion in order to keep good faith with their clients and repaid them their money at his own expense, so the whole family moved to the beach house at Manly.

This included Alfred and his wife Harriet, and their three daughters, Alice, Violet and my grandmother Harriet Gwenyth Newmarch, and her three chidren, Patricia, Joy and my father Colin Alfred Chapman. My grandmother had left her husband after she discovered that he had gambled away a substantial amount of her property. This led to a close relationship between my father Colin and his grandfather Alfred, who became the dominant male influence and role model in his life. Also residing in the High Street residence were Violet's husband and their daughter Gwen.

That was a little aside, but back now to Alfred's forebears, and the links with York.

Henry Fowler Newmarch, Alfred's father, was also born in India to Dr Henry Newmarch, an assistant surgeon in the 2nd Brigade Horse Artillery, and Violet Sherwood who was born in Bengal, (Calcutta), in 1803. I believe her father was Captain James Doddington Sherwood, and her mother is recorded simply as 'Mary', (India Office, The British Library). I had been unable to find any birth or marriage records for

C1930 Dad Aged about 4 years with his grandfather Alfred Newmarch with the T Model Ford.Outside the Family Beachhouse

C 1934 Family Camping Holiday. Alfred far left, Mary his Wife (My great grandmother) is far right Colin Alfred (my Dad) next to Alfred.

'Mary', and suspected that she may have been an Indian woman, as many British Officers had liaisons with Indian women, and produced so many children, that "The Military Orphan House", Calcutta, was built and funded by the British officers, to house and educate the children, who were actually not orphans! The funding was by a system of monthly contributions from the officers. (British Library, India Office).

The original home was built on the west banks of the River Hooghly, at Howrah, near Calcutta, then, in 1790, the 'orphanage' moved to 'Kidderpore', in Calcutta. Margaret McMillan, in her book, "Women of the Raj", explains that, the Kidderpore Orphanage, was mainly for daughters of British Officers and Indian women, and monthly balls were held, where bachelors could find wives, and it was the responsibility of the headmistress, to 'marry off' the girls!

I had no absolute proof of the assertion that Mary was Indian, however, it would have explained my great grandfather's 'suntanned complexion'! In the early '70s I spent seven and a half months in India, and travelled to Simla and Mussourie, hill stations where some of the Newmarch children are recorded as having been born, and even though my grandmother was alive at the time, neither she nor my father 'let out' the family secret, that my great grandfather, and his father and his siblings were born there, and indeed, another generation before them, lived in India.

This romantic notion has now been quashed as I have received information from the Librarian at the British Library India Office, that Mary, (Violet's mother), was definitely a white European woman, and married James in Calcutta on 15/12/1795. Her brother, David Thomas Richardson, was also a Bengal Army Officer. This information is corroborated by Henry and Violet's youngest son, Oliver's middle name being, "Richardson", Violet's maiden name.

Dr Henry Newmarch, arrived in India on 14th November, 1818, aboard the HMS "Northumberland". Amazingly, Napoleon Bonaparte was transported on this very same ship from Plymouth to St. Helena, a tiny dot of an island in the Atlantic Ocean, 5,000 miles from England, where he was exiled, in 1815. HMS 'Northumberland', was then one of three Flagships stationed at St Helena during the exile, and was there from December 1815, until June 1816, (The National Archives, *Napoleon on St Helena')*.

Dr Henry Newmarch had gone to serve as an assistant surgeon for the East India Company which controlled and payrolled the Bengal Army, which was basically a private army, and was there to protect the assets of the Company.

Henry was the second son of Joseph Newmarch and Honor Ward, who were married in the church of St Martin, Coney Street, York, on 26th April, 1779. Another of Joseph and Honor's children, was George Newmarch, who with his wife Mary, were the parents of Charles Henry and George Frederick, the authors of The Newmarch Pedigree.

Micklegate was a narrow winding street, overlooked on both sides by two and three storey buildings, some leaning into the way. Within a few hundred metres, I reached The Priory Church of Holy Trinity Micklegate, where some of Joseph and Honor's children were baptized including Henry

Holy Trinity Micklegate

(Dr), in 1798, and George, in 1791, Sarah in 1792, and Joseph in 1795. The churchyard was shaded by old oak trees, which partly obscured the outline of the church, and fallen leaves littered the damp path. As I entered the dimly lit sanctuary, the exultant strains of organ music filled and awakened the space, and were quite wonderful.

I sat in the pew trying to fathom the fact that my ancestors were here in this place over two hundred years ago, which was incredible. The Monks of Micklegate were here over eight hundred years ago, which was explained by an exhibition of their history. Beautiful arrangements of fruit and flowers decorated the entry for Harvest Festival.

Emerging once more into the natural, though dull light, I continued down Micklegate and crossed the bridge over the River Ouse, which flows eventually into the mighty Humber, and into the North Sea. Several old warehouses remain, at the water's edge, a reminder of the importance of the river in times past as it conveyed vessels filled with goods from near and far.

At the bottom of the hill I turned left into Coney Street, and not much further on, was the famous clock of St. Martin, Coney Street Church, which hung out over the footpath on the outstretched arm of an ornate cantilevered cast iron frame. On top of the handsome black and gold clock, stood a herald dressed in 18th century attire, (similar to the clothing which history books depict Captain Cook wearing).

This was the church where Joseph and Honor Newmarch were married in 1779. The closed small access door in the main oak gothic entrance door, bore the sign:

"KEEP PIGEONS OUT

AND PEACE WITHIN.

PLEASE CLOSE THE DOOR."

Remnants of streamers escaped from the top of that little door, and above it was a warning on a large red sign:

'MIND YOUR HEAD'.

Duly warned and instructed, I ducked as I entered the surprisingly light space, where several women were consumed in preparations for some special event, so I wandered through the relatively small space almost unnoticed. A sign at the gate reported that the church was partly destroyed during a WW11 bombing raid, in 1942, and a section of it had been rebuilt in 1968. I believe that the section where Joseph and Honor were married was no longer there, however I was still standing in the place where they made their vows in 1779.

Curiously, whilst researching the family, I noticed that following their marriage on 26th April, 1779, Joseph and Honor had no family until George was born, and baptized on 7/1/1791, almost twelve years later! Then followed a procession of children:

George	7/1/1791
Sarah	8/4/1792
Joseph	26/6/1795
Harriott	1/11/1796
Henry	23/2/1798
Honor	23/8/1799
Marion	9/2/1802

St Martin's Coney Street, York

135

- Seven children in eleven years, after twelve years of nothing! Why did it take so long to start the family?   I wondered if Joseph was a soldier, and had gone to war, or was perhaps he was absent for some other reason?

Searching for some answers to these intriguing questions, I kept walking under my newly purchased umbrella, to the YORK ARCHIVES, which were housed in the York City Library.

The archivist directed me to the card catalogue, where I found several references to 'Newmarches'. Some of the older references were too old to be on Microfiche, and the assistant kindly went down to the Archives and returned with 2 huge volumes, which contained 'broadsheet' newspapers from the 1790's. With gloved hands she carefully turned the two hundred and twenty year old pages to reveal some very interesting details.

Joseph Newmarch was advertising in the "York Herald", as early as 27th October, 1792 as being, 'Without Mickelgate Bar', in other words, he was situated outside the city walls, on Mickelgate Street, and was advertising himself as a 'wine and spirit merchant, and tea dealer'.

Then followed advertisements in the 'York Herald' on, 14/3/1795, and 3/3/1798, for the lease of his house, giving a wonderful description, as follows, in old English, with then 'long S' in use, which makes some of the 'S's look like 'F's. Confusingly, only some of the S's are long. I have no idea why, but will reproduce the text as given, thus:

YORK

To be LET

"A Large genteel, well-built DWELLING
HOUSE, with fpacious cellars and
convenient outbuildings, being in a very airy and
pleafant fituation without Micklegate Bar, and now
inhabited by Mr Jofeph Newmarch, Wine-Merchant;
together with a commodious Warehoufe,
and Wine-Vaults under the fame, a Yard, Stabling
for three horfes, and a very good Garden, well flored
with a variety of choice fruit-trees.
The premifes may be viewed, and particulars
known, on application to Mr. Newmarch on the
premifes."

The assistant explained to me that this would have
been in a very 'well to do' area along near the racecourse,
where the road is wide and treelined.

I later discovered that the centre of the city near 'The
Shambles', was putrid with flies, the stench of rotting meat
and disease, where blood flowed and soured in the streets
as butchers slaughtered livestock for the meat market.
This made living 'without Micklegate', all the more desirable
and only for the privileged.

either of the York Banks.

YORK.

To be LET,

For the remainder of a Leafe, fix years and a half or thirteen years and a half of which are unexpired, and may be entered on at May-Day next,

A Large, genteel, well-built DWEL-LING HOUSE, with fpacious cellars and convenient outbuildings, being in a very airy and pleafant fituation without Micklegate Bar, and now inhabited by Mr. Jofeph Newmarch, Wine-Merchant; together with a commodious Warehoufe, and Wine-Vaults under the fame, a Yard, Stabling for three horfes, and a very good Garden, well ftored with a variety of choice fruit-trees.

The premifes may be viewed, and particulars known, on application to Mr. NEWMARCH on the premifes.

To be SOLD,

York Herald Advertisement from 1795

Quite a large advertisement was placed in the 'York Herald', on the 19th October, 1799, which made me wonder if Joseph Newmarch had been on the high seas to the 'East" during those twelve years before the family began in 1791.

"YORK,

Saturday – Oct. 19.

JOSEPH NEWMARCH,

At his Tea, Sugar, and Spice Warehoufe,

(IMPORTER OF SPIRITOUS LIQUORS)

Returns his fincere Thanks to his Friends

And the Public for paft Favours, and begs leave to

Inform them that having attended the LAST EAST

INDIA SALE, he has felected a large Assortment of

TEAS,

Of the fineft QUALITY and FLAVOUR, which he

Will fell on the moft REASONABLE TERMS; and

having been frequently applied to for

SUGARS,

He has, in compliance with the wifhes of his Friends,

commenced the Sale of that Article, which he is

determined to fell at the moft REDUCED PRICES,

and of the BEST QUALITY.

having alfo purchafed a Quantity of CLOVES,

MACE, CINNAMON, and NUTMEGS, he folicits the Orders of

his Friends for thofe Articles,

which will be fold much lower than they have lately been.

***COFFEE, CHOCOLATE, and QUEEN's

GENUINE PATENT COCOA,

at the Loweft Prices.

GOOD LUMP SUGAR,   1s. per lb.

GOOD RAW SUGAR,   8p. per lb."

———*———

This was an amazing find, and I wondered if this link with the East India Company was the catalyst for his son, Henry going to India as a doctor with the East India Company? This 'touching the exotic', in England at the end of the 18th century, may also have influenced Joseph's grandson, and Henry's nephew, Charles Henry Newmarch, co author of, 𝕿𝖍𝖊 𝕹𝖊𝖜𝖒𝖆𝖗𝖈𝖍 𝕻𝖊𝖉𝖎𝖌𝖗𝖊𝖊, who I have now discovered authored two volumes entitled, "Five Years in the East". In this work, he recounts his adventures whilst sailing to many lands in East Asia, including India and China, beginning in 1844 when he was just 20 years of age. He explains in the preface of, Volume 1, that the five years is a misnomer, and that the 'five years', could be compressed into three years, which is why the books could, and were published in 1847.

I was very excited to find these volumes, and remembered that Phillip at Belton, (where Charles had served as the Vicar for 37 years), had said that he believed that Charles had written other books: and here they were! It's interesting that they were printed in Cirencester, where Charles' brother George, worked as a solicitor.

Besides '𝓕𝓲𝓿𝓮 𝓨𝓮𝓪𝓻𝓼 𝓲𝓷 𝓽𝓱𝓮 𝓔𝓪𝓼𝓽 𝓥𝓸𝓵𝓾𝓶𝓮𝓼 1 & 11', Charles also co-authored, "Illustrations of the Remains of Roman Art in Cirencester, the Site of Antient Corinium", with Prof. Buckman, Cirencester, which was published in 1850, as noted earlier, so I therefore believe that it is reasonable to assume that Charles was the primary writer of 𝕿𝖍𝖊 𝕹𝖊𝖜𝖒𝖆𝖗𝖈𝖍 𝕻𝖊𝖉𝖎𝖌𝖗𝖊𝖊.

YORK,

SATURDAY—OCT. 19.

JOSEPH NEWMARCH,

At his Tea, Sugar, and Spice Warehouse,

(IMPORTER OF SPIRITUOUS LIQUORS.)

RETURNS his sincere Thanks to his FRIENDS and the PUBLIC for past Favours, and begs leave to inform them that having attended the LAST EAST INDIA SALE, he has selected a large ASSORTMENT of

TEAS,

of the finest QUALITY and FLAVOUR, which he will sell on the most REASONABLE TERMS; and having been frequently applied to for

SUGARS,

he has, in compliance with the wishes of his Friends, commenced the Sale of that Article, which he is determined to sell at the most REDUCED PRICES, and of the BEST QUALITY.

Having also purchased a Quantity of CLOVES, MACE, CINNAMON, and NUTMEGS, he solicits the Orders of his Friends for those Articles, which will be sold much lower than they have lately been.

* COFFEE, CHOCOLATE, and QUEEN'S GENUINE PATENT COCOA, at the Lowest Prices.

GOOD LUMP SUGAR,	1s. per lb.
GOOD RAW SUGAR,	8½. per lb.

The 1799 Advertisement in The York Herald

Now back to my finds in the York Archives after that digression. I found three death notices. The archivist explained that only very wealthy people could afford newspaper death notices in those days.

The first was in the 'York Herald', in the death notices, 23rd December, 1816: *"Yesterday morning, in the 58th year of her age, Mrs. Newmarch, wife of Mr. Newmarch, late of this City."* This was Honor, born on 22nd November, 1757.

The next notice appeared in the *'York Herald & General Advertiser'*, on *Saturday October 18th, 1823: "On Tuesday, at Altrincham, in his 77th year of his age, Mr. Newmarch. Late of this city."* This was Joseph Newmarch born 10th August, 1747 in Wrawby, Lincolnshire, Honor's husband.

The 'York Gazette', on 30th June, 1866, printed this death notice: *"NEWMARCH – On the 22nd instant, at 74 Micklegate, in this city, aged 68 years, Henry Newmarch, Esq., M.D., late surgeon Bengal Army."*

So Henry had returned from India. This raised more questions, such as; was he there for the Indian Mutiny? How many of the family stayed in India? One interesting fact had emerged, and that was that he lived at 74 Micklegate, which I had walked right past that morning, and I would find on the way back to the Convent!

On further research, I discovered, that Dr. Henry, then aged 53years of age, appears on the 1851 England Census records, without his wife Violet, and is recorded as a, 'lodger', at 24 Clifton Street, Clifton, Yorkshire, along with his unmarried, 27 year old daughter Violet. She was the eldest child, with four brothers, Charles Douglas, Henry Fowler,

74 Micklegate, the Home of Dr Henry Newmarch in 1866

(my great, great grandfather), George, and Oliver Richardson, and, as I have recently discovered, a much younger sister Mary Caroline, who was the only child not born in India, and was in fact born in France, and baptised at the British Chapel, Boulogne-Sur-Mer, pas de Calais, France. She was eighteen years younger than her older sister Violet!

At least three of the brothers, were highly ranked and decorated Officers in the Bengal Army, with Oliver, being made a Knight-Commander of the Order of the Star of India, and serving as, Major-General Sir Oliver Richardson Newmarch, Military Secretary to the India Office, from 1889-1899.

In the 1861 England Census records, Dr Henry, now 63 years old, and still with his unmarried daughter, Violet (now 37 years), is recorded as being a boarder, at 26 Old Elvit Road, St. Oswald, Durham. Violet, his wife, is now in England, and appears in the same 1861 England Census, at Hampstead, Middlesex, occupation, 'fundholder'. She is listed as a 'visitor', and accompanied by her eighteen year old daughter, Caroline.

By the 1871 England Census, Dr Henry, had died at his home in York in 1866, and the widowed Violet, now 68 years old, and seemingly settled at, 20 Colville Terrace East, Kensington Park, London, is recorded as the 'head of household', Occupation, Annuitant. Her spinster daughter Violet is now with her, and also her youngest son, 36 year old, recently widowed, Captain Oliver Richardson Newmarch. His wife, Mary Isabella Parke, died that year, leaving behind, four young daughters aged from four to twelve years.

Probate records show that Violet died at the same Kensington Park address four years later, on 18th July, 1875, where Violet her daughter, is named as the Guardian of her niece, Janie Parke Newmarch, Oliver's youngest daughter.

I stepped back into the 21st century, onto the rain soaked pavements of York, and made for the towering spires of York Minster. The 'Minster' was amazing, and so vast. Crowds swarmed through the largest Gothic church north of the Alps in awe and wonder, exclaiming at the beauty of the sanctuary. Suddenly I was aware of a priest's voice, which I soon discovered was coming from a side chapel, where fifty or so people were gathered to partake of the midday Holy Communion Service. I filled a vacant seat, and shared in a heart warming service with other like minded Christians, thrilled that I was able to have such a wonderful experience in such an incredible place.

Heartened, and grateful for the continuing blessings that were coming my way, I joined the line, outside the famous, 'Betty's Tea Rooms', where I was sure my late mother, Betty, would have visited on her trip here in the '80s. The wait was worth it, as I enjoyed one of 'Betty's' famed 'Afternoon Teas', served on a tiered platter, complete with all manner of delicacies, including dainty quartered sandwiches of beef & mustard, egg, crab and chicken, a fruit scone with strawberry jam and clotted cream, a raspberry tart, macaroon, chocolate cake, and lots of Betty's special tea blend, all served on fine china, and a silver tea pot. The passers by on the square's wet cobblestones, could be seen through the curved glass corner wall. At length I joined them, replete and happy.

As I followed the signage to, 'The Shambles', I stumbled upon a tour group, where the guide was beginning an interesting commentary on the city. I asked him if it was a paid tour, and he told me it was a 'Package Tour', then asked me if I was on my own. I replied in the affirmative, and he kindly invited me to join the group!

We snaked our way through the narrow winding, cobbled alleyways, which were 'The Shambles'. A sign explained that it was the ancient street of the Butchers of York, and, *"took its name from the word, 'shamel' meaning the stalls or benches on which the meat was displayed"*. It must have been loathsome for those who lived there in the conditions I described earlier.

We continued on, hearing stories of depraved poverty and unbelievable living conditions, and stories of mad prostitutes, as we walked through the dark claustrophobic, 'Lund's Court', formerly, known as 'Mad Alice's Lane'. We wandered through the marketplace, and eventually into open space, where the guide gave meeting instructions for the members of the group.

The rain continued as I retraced my steps to 74 Micklegate, the home of Dr Henry Newmarch. The brown brick three storey building, in a row of terraces, was on the curve of the narrow road, as I walked up the gentle rise. Shops occupied the ground floor of all the buildings along Mickelgate.

Signage on No. 74 boasts "The French House", however the building was currently empty, and available for lease. I

Betty's Tea Rooms

was fortunate to find an interesting, recently published book, from Spelman's Bookshop next door, at 70 & 72 Mickelgate. "Looking Back at Micklegate, Nunnery Lane & Bishophill, York" by Avril E. Webster Appleton, which gives an historic account of the area, and in fact has a photo of No. 74, and explains that it had been a bakery in 1932, owned by the Woodcock family. The bakery was so successful, that they had made two fruitcakes in 1965, for the Royal Garden Party, and were finalists in a competition to find Britain's best baker. The author goes on to say that No. 74 Micklegate later became 'Wills Brothers & Ribble Paint Shop, (page 163-164). What a day I'd had! Through the continuing rain, I reflected on yet another wonderful day, as I walked the short distance to the Bar Convent,

Chapter XIV

Next morning I left a very damp York, travelling past stately homes on Mickelgate, which was the area where the archivist had suggested that Joseph Newmarch's house would have been. Through metronomic windscreen wipers, and heavy rain, I peered, wondering which of these was the home in question.

With no answers, and left to ponder, I continued due south down the A1 to Womersley, once known as Wymersley, and referred to as such in *The Newmarch Pedigree*.

Reference to Womersley first appears on *Page* 4, in relation to Ralph de Newmarch, son of Bernard de Newmarch, who we have already made reference to as being a companion of Roger de Busli, and in relation to 'the Honour of Tickhill', and as having knights fees in A.D. 1088. *"Among his possessions in this county of York were Bentley-cum-Arksey, near Doncaster, where he had his mansion, Bolton, Wymersley, and Barnby-upon-Don..."*.

The next reference on *Page* 9, is in relation to Adam de Newmarch 3rd who, five generations further on from Ralph, still *"held Bentley-cum-Arksey, and other knight's fees of the Honour of Tickhill belonging to the Newmarch Family, Wymersley, Campsall, Thorne in Balne, and other manors in the counties of York and Lincoln"*.

Just to recap: this is the same Adam de Newmarch who in A.D. 1263, *"advanced his banner in open rebellion against the King at Northampton.....his manors of Bentley,*

Wymersley, Campsall, and Thorne, Co. York, and all his lands in the county of Lincoln were then seized under the King's warrant, and committed to the charge of Richard Foliat", (Page 10).

Adam de Newmarch 3rd, was then involved in the Seige of Kenilworth, and obtained restitution of his estates under the 'Dictum of Kenilworth', *"though, probably with limited control of his power, and the deprivation of his son, in favour of his daughter and her issue",* (Page 11).

Because of this 'Dictum of Kenilworth', when Adam 3rd died in A.D. 1276, most of his lands passed to the Tibetots, through his daughter Eva, who had married Robert Tibetot. However, Wymersley, Warmsworth, and some other manors, were retained by the family, under some arrangement made, to make provision for his son and heir Adam 4th, who married Elizabeth, daughter of Roger de Mowbray, (Page 12).

Adam 4th's second son Roger, succeeded his father after the death of his childless brother John, and was involved in the Scottish Wars, in A.D.1314. Subsequently, four years later, King Edward 11 granted him *"Freewarren in all his lands in Wilmersley or Wymersley, Rishingthorp, Askern, and Scunthorpe in Co. York",* (Page 14). This basically meant that he had hunting rights in those lands.

The Newmarch Pedigree, Page 15, states that his son, Roger de Newmarch 2nd, was a *"loyal and trusted subject"* of King Edward 111, and in A.D. 1347, *"he had granted him a charter for a weekly market, and a fair on St.Martin's Eve in his manor at Wymersley".*

Charles Newmarch lastly cites Hunter writing in 1828, saying that, *"a fine monumental effigy of this Knight is still to be seen in the church of Wymersley, in the windows of which were once the figures of Ralph de Newmarch, and Elizabeth his wife"*.

Against this monumental backdrop of history, I turned off the A1, and approached Womersley. Two things were apparent. Firstly, high stonewalls, probably at least 10 or 12 feet high, on both sides of the road, went for miles! Secondly, I didn't see a person. The village seemed deserted, but perhaps the populace was staying indoors out of the rain, or, were hidden behind the endless stonewalls. Eventually I reached the Church of St Martin, which was set back from the road, where the high stonewalls continued up the laneway.

As I hadn't seen a person I was holding my breath and praying that the church would be open, and it was! I stepped inside what I discovered to be a 12th century, "magnesian" limestone church, with a 13th century north aisle, which was full of Newmarch history!

Wonderfully, the full size cross-legged stone Knight effigy, was there, and, according to the sign, dates from the 13th century, and was named as Adam de Newmarch. He is holding his sword, and a shield bearing the Newmarch coat of arms, of 'Five Fussils in Fesse', and wearing chain mail.

It was quite 'jaw dropping' to stand there before this ancient physical remnant of family history.

However The Newmarch Pedigree, Page 15, cites Hunter, who in 1828, believed this to be Roger de Newmarch 2nd, as

The Stone Knight Effigy in Womersley Church

mentioned above. Interestingly, above the knight, in stone, is the Newmarch shield, showing quartered arms for Sir Robert Newmarch. His father Sir Ralph Newmarch of Wymersley, married his mother Elizabeth Newmarch, of Whatton in A.D.1377, thus bringing the two branches of the Newmarch family back together, hence the quartered arms.

It is the figures of these Sir Ralph, and Elizabeth, which have been mentioned as at one time being in the windows of this church. As to the windows of the church, a framed document, hung in the church, entitled,

"As Recorded by Dodsworth in 1621

The Heraldry in the Windows of Womersley Church".

Of the ten shields represented, seven of those bore the Newmarch 'Five fussils in fesse', one of those was quartered with 'Ardene', one shield was John Neville of Womersley, and the other was the rampant Lion of Mowbray. Unfortunately, none of the original windows remain, but I was elated to find that historical documentation.

The altar area and choir stalls, were divided from the main body of the church by elaborate iron gates, which bore a sign, which read, 'Alarmed'! Skeptical as to the truth of the matter, I deliberated as to whether I would put it to the test, but fearful of causing mayhem in this silent community, I controlled my curiosity, and left, very content that I'd been able to enter at all, and to have seen so much.

There were quite a few very large old stone buildings near the church, and I wondered if they had been part of the manor. Later I remembered that Joyce, the local history expert at the church at Althorp, had given me a booklet

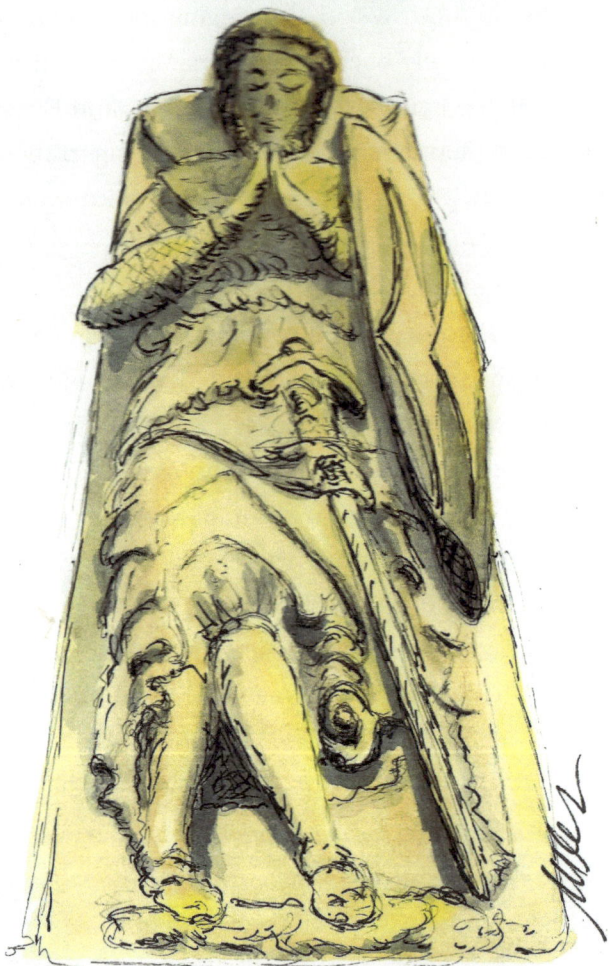

13th Century Stone Knight Effigy of Adam de Newmarch, or is it Roger de Newmarch 2nd?

The Abundant Newmarch Heraldry in the Church Windows at Wymersley as recorded by Dodsworth in 1621

entitled, "The Wood Hall Moated Manor Project ... 1000 years of Country Life in Yorkshire". Apparently, this project was undertaken by the North Yorkshire County Council, and supported by National Power, as a two year archeological assessment project, of the 'Wood Hall Manor' which I now know is situated one mile north of Womersley village.

According to page 6 of the booklet, the Manor of Womersley, which was part of the Honour of Pontrefract, passed into the hands of the de Newmarch family, in 1183, when the heiress of Otes de Tilley, who owned lands in Askern and Doncaster, married into the Newmarch family,

The document goes on to explain, that it was probably *"one of them"*, who ordered that the moat be dug as a defensive measure, and, *"when Wood Hall is first mentioned in documents in 1327/28, it was owned by Queen Isabella, the wife of King Edward 11, and held by the de Newmarch family. Wood Hall was a small manor, carved out of the woods of Womersley"*.

And again on Page 10, *"In the mid fifteenth century the ownership of Womersley and wood Hall changed through marriage. The de Newmarch heiress, Elizabeth, married John Neville of Althorpe in Lincolnshire. Their daughter Joan married Sir William Gascoigne......Wood Hall remained in the possession of the Gascoignes through the sixteenth century"*.

Unfortunately, I missed seeing the archeological site, but with the weather as it was, I may not have missed much!

My next destination was Nostell Priory, which was about a half hour or so drive to the west of Womersley, which entailed zig-zagging cross-country, on an indirect mesh of roads, through continuing rain.

Nostell Priory is first mentioned in The Newmarch Pedigree, Page 4. Here, Adam de Newmarch 1st, grandson of Bernard de Newmarch, (Neufmarche), and successor of his father Ralph, *"is known as the benefactor of the House of Austin, Canons of Nostell Co. York, Temp Henry 1, (A.D. 1135) which was repaired at that time, (Camd. Brit. 851)"*.

The text goes on to say that Adam married Lady Adelina of Whatton, Notts, who, *"Made a gift to the Canons of Nostell, of lands in Whatton"*. Further, *"Adam de Newmarch 2nd, son of Henry, and grandson of Adam 1st, benefactor of Nostell, and is recorded to have confirmed the gift which Adelina had made to that house of lands in Whatton, probably in the reign of Henry 111, circa A.D. 1216"*, (Page 8).

A further reference on Page 17, tells us confusingly of another Adam de Newmarch, younger son of Adam 2nd, who succeeded his father in the possession of the Whatton Estates, and was the uncle and contemporary of the 3rd Adam de Newmarch (son of Robert), of the 'Seige of Kenilworth' fame:

"He is recorded to have confirmed the gifts of his ancestors, Adam and Adelina, to the Canons of Nostell, an act which serves to identify him and prove his descent".

"Nostell Priory & Parkland", is now a National Trust property, and the paying visitors car park, is several hundred metres from the buildings. I paid my money to the car park machine, which spat out a windscreen ticket, and

An Newer Building at Nostell Priory

then proceeded along the path, which curved along the top of a rolling meadow. Eventually I reached a gate, and could venture no further, not even to the Gift Shop or toilet, as today was Tuesday, and today Nostell Priory was closed! In the distance, I could see a handsome manor house, and to the left older stone buildings with a huge courtyard and spire, which was currently undergoing refurbishment. Stable blocks were even further back obscured by leafy oak trees, and ancient stonewalls.

I was disappointed not to have been able to explore this historic site more fully, but having no option but to take long-distance photos, I did just that, and returned in drizzle to the car park. I consoled myself with a cup of tea in the local pub, for a whole 85p, before backtracking to Campsall.

The same trademark interminable, high walls, which were a feature of Womersley, were also present at Campsall, which is mentioned in The Newmarch Pedigree, Page 9, in relation to Adam de Newmarch 3rd, (of Siege of Kenilworth fame), as one of the, *"knight's fees of the Honor of Tickhill belonging to the Newmarch family"*, along with, *"Wymersley, Thorne, Thorpe in Balne, and other manors in the counties of York and Lincoln"*. It is also mentioned on Page 10, as one of the manors seized under the King's warrant, as previously mentioned.

The Parish Church of St. Mary Magdalene, stood imposing and silent. The wonderful exotically patterned gothic oak door was locked, so I was left to wander the churchyard and contemplate the history of the family here at Campsall.

On the rise, across the road, behind the high stonewall, the top of another ecclesiastically oriented building, (which I suspected was the rectory or vicarage), could be seen through leafy old oak trees. Someone peered at me from an upper window, but offered no help, as to the story of Campsall.

I drove the short distance to Askern, which is recorded in 𝕿𝖍𝖊 𝕹𝖊𝖜𝖒𝖆𝖗𝖈𝖍 𝕻𝖊𝖉𝖎𝖌𝖗𝖊𝖊, 𝕻𝖆𝖌𝖊 14, as being one of the places where, Roger de Newmarch, who had served King Edward 11, in the Scottish wars, was granted by the King, in A.D. 1318, *"Freewarren in all his lands"*.

At last there were some signs of life, there were shops, there were people, and the treed landscape broadened to reveal a lake where ducks and geese, nonchalantly moved across the surface, or waddled in patrols around the promenade, in search of tit bits from those few individuals, who had come out to enjoy the brief sunshine.

I was pleasantly surprised to find 'The Lake Café', which was situated adjacent to the promenade on the lakefront. I joined some locals who were tucking into delicious home cooked meals at reasonable prices. Mine was deliciously hot, mince and onion pie, with carrots, peas, mashed potato and gravy, which warmed body and soul, before I headed to the south of England.

Chapter XV

I drove through leafy oak forests in East Sussex, where I imagined that Robin Hood would have been right at home, before arriving at the town of 'Battle', the site of the momentous 'Battle of Hastings'.

The main street of Battle was so congested with traffic on that fine morning, that a small policewoman had taken charge of the mayhem and was endeavouring to prevent Battle from coming to a complete standstill! At the end of the main street, towering above the traffic jam, the ancient russet stone turrets of the Battle Abbey Great Gatehouse, and attached Courthouse, were outlined against the azure backdrop of the beautiful morning.

A crowd was gathering on the cobbled concourse outside the entry point to Battle Abbey and the battlefield beyond, waiting for the clock to tick over to the magic opening hour.

The Newmarch Pedigree begins on Page 1 with, *"Bernard de Novo Mercatu, Neofmarche, or Newmarch, accompanied William the Conqueror on his invading England, A.D. 1066"*, and, *"Bernard de Newmarch fought at Hastings. His name appears on the roll of Battle Abbey, and he was one of the witnesses to King William's Charter to the Monks of Battle. (Dugd. Monast. 1, 317). A facsimile of his signature is given in the Autographic Mirror, Vol. 2, No. 20."*

William Duke of Normandy, was a tough man, and had endured personal battles to hold that title. He was born at Falaise, in Normandy, France in A.D. 1027, the son of

Battle Abbey Great Gate House

Seal of Battle Abbey

'Robert the Magnificent', who had converted to Catholicism, but still maintained the Viking tradition of having a mistress as well as a wife in the castle, where the illegitimate children of those liaisons, shared equal status with the legitimate children.

'William the Bastard', or 'the bastard King', were terms which dogged his life, and made him even more determined to thwart his enemies and to prove his worth. Before Edward the Confessor, King of England, died in A.D. 1064, he named William Duke of Normandy as his successor to the English throne. This came about because Edward the Confessor's mother, Queen Emma, was the daughter of Duke Richard of Normandy, and thus William's great aunt, ("Battle Abbey and Battlefield", English Heritage, Page 8).

Edward sent his brother-in-law, Harold to Normandy to convey the news to William, however, Harold was blown off course, and captured, and taken to the Duke of Normandy for a ransom, where he swore an oath of allegiance to William, assuring him that he would be King. Shortly after Harold returned to England, King Edward died, and Harold himself was crowned King of England on 6th January, 1066.

On hearing news of this, an enraged William set about quickly, but methodically preparing to take back the Crown which he believed to be rightly his. He firstly, sent emissaries to Rome to seek the blessing of the Pope, and was granted 'The Standard of St Peter', which he proudly carried into battle, ("William the Conqueror", Anne Fetta, p.14). In the next few months, over five hundred vessels were built and prepared, and after a false start, due to bad weather, the fleet, carrying 12 – 15,000 men, and around 3,000 horses, along with arms and provisions, landed on the south coast of England at Pevensey, on the 29th September, 1066, ("William the Conqueror", Fetta P.16).

William planned to march north to London from Pevensey, and on 13th October 1066, they had camped at the foot of Battle Hill, which was about 15 miles north east of Pevensey, and just 7 miles north of Hastings, the English Channel seaside town. Harold, hearing of their arrival, had advanced his troops south after defeating the Vikings at York, and met the invading forces the next morning, on the 14th October, 1066, and the battle began.

Harold's forces took up positions at the top of the rise, giving them an advantage over the invaders. However, armed with just shields and battle axes, they were no match for the might of William's army, who were mobile, protected by chain-mail, and they had a combination of archers, infantrymen armed with javelins, and two to three thousand horsemen.

By the end of the day the battle was over. Harold, who had received an arrow in the eye, was dead, along with his two brothers, and around 7,000 others! Any surviving Saxons had fled. Today I surveyed verdant pasture, which stretched peacefully into the morning, across the flat to distant oak trees, where birds chirped happily on that glorious morning.

So here I was, overlooking the battlefield where Bernard had fought that day, I imagined as one of the knights on horseback. I was probably close to where Harold's men were positioned for battle, as the recorded commentary on my headset painted a vivid picture of the bloodthirsty battle. Suddenly, the magical imagery of the moment was shattered as out of nowhere, two white vans drove across the lush battlefield. Being catapulted back into the present, I realized that in only two days time, it would be October 14th, the anniversary of the Battle of Hastings, and so, preparations were underway in readiness for a full scale reenactment.

I turned my attention to the remains of the cluster of stone monastic buildings, which lay on the ridge above the battlefield. Immediately behind the Terrace Walk, were the impressively high stonewalls and ramparts of the double storey "East Range", which housed the monastic dormitory, the latrines, the common room, and the novices' chamber, which was on the ground floor. Enormous, and cold, her walls, emerald green with moss in places, (on the inside), cradled the novices' chamber, which sported a wonderful stone, fan vaulted ceiling, which was supported by Sussex marble pillars on an earthy stone floor. The huge monastic dormitory above, now roofless, was not accessible to visit, but the dimensions could be appreciated when viewed through the absent north wall!

Close by, was the site of the Chapter House and the former Abbey Church and crypt, and the cloister, which led to the amazing ecclesiastical buildings, now making up, 'Battle Abbey School'. It was Anthea, who I had met in Llangasty in Wales, who had told me that she had gone to school at 'Battle Abbey', and to whom I was indebted for my being there. The "Abbey School", which was the

The Site where the Battle of Hastings took Place in 1066

167

dominating feature on the top of the hill, was made up of the wonderful castellated buildings, which were formerly the West Range, and the Abbot's Lodging.

William the Conqueror established The Benedictine Abbey of Battle, on becoming King William 1, to celebrate his victory over Harold, and to fulfill his Papal obligations. He endowed it richly and Battle Abbey flourished as one of the richest monasteries in England for 400 years until the dissolution of the monasteries under King Henry V111. It may be worthwhile at this point, to recall that following the death of William 1 in A.D. 1087, when Bernard invaded Brecknockshire, in Wales, that he founded a Benedictine Priory in Brecon, *"which he liberally endowed, and constituted a cell to Battle Abbey, in memory of his first wife Agnes"*, (Ƈɧe Ոewmarcɧ Ԃeɗigree, Ԃage 2ʹ3). This is an interesting link, no doubt perpetuated by Roger Monk of Battle, and perhaps it was in deference and loyalty to his former companion, and King, William 1.

As I wandered around the grounds of the Abbey, I visited the 19th century ice house, then made my way between hedgerows and the 'Precinct Wall' to the towered gatehouse, where the souvenir shop had a poster of "The Roll of Battle Abbey", upon which I found the name of "Neofmarche".

Satisfied with the morning's wonderful physical history lesson, I walked out through the amazing Great Gatehouse, and across the road to 'The Pilgrims' Rest', an extraordinary Tudor style 'Wealden Hall House' dating from A.D. 1420.

Inside the Novices' Chamber Battle Abbey

The Monastic Dormitory Battle Abbey

Former Abbot's Lodgings - Now rear of Battle Abbey School.
The Site of the Cloisters is in the Foreground

This style of house is characterized by exposed oak frame, and whitewashed walls filled with earth, dung and horsehair, jettied or overhanging first floor and a steep pitched roof. In the case of 'The Pilgrims' Rest, the roof was shingled, but I imagine it would have been originally thatched.

Pastel roses in full bloom, welcomed all comers between the gate and the house. Walking through the wide gothic front door into the dimly lit, but large space, one was overtaken by an amazing sense of history. A fire blazed in the enormous fireplace, which legend has it, was the entrance to a secret passageway, which led to the Abbey across the road! I loved the ambience as I enjoyed a good old 'Cream Tea', what we in Australia would call, a 'Devonshire Tea' – scones with cream and strawberry jam, and a pot of tea!

Replete, I drove the short distance through wooded farmland to Pevensey, the site of the Norman landing. A perfectly flat, calm English Channel met the stony beach, whose timber groins, meant to prevent the erosive effects of a relentless sea, were barely visible above the accumulated stones.

I followed the coast road to Hastings, and checked into one of the many four storey hotels, which stood shoulder to shoulder in a seemingly never ending line of buildings, which mirrored the Channel-hugging promenade across the road.

From my attic room balcony, I looked out over the Channel, and the sad site of the recently burnt out Hastings Pier. That night, a full moon illuminated the crashing waves

The Pilgrims' Rest Tearooms

of the relentless incoming tide, and with the invigorating sea breeze filling my room, I slept soundly.

Chapter XVI

I woke to a bright sunny morning, and after a good breakfast, I set off to travel the fifty or so miles to Dover. Despite sunshine at sea level, as the road climbed high over the cliffs, heavy fog and low cloud descended, reducing visibility.

The morning was full of surprises as I passed the very odd shaped oast houses, or hop kilns with their cone shaped roofs. Then I reached the little town of Rye which was abuzz as it was obviously market day, and everyone was in town.

From Rye, I took the low road through the marshlands and low farming country, and actually passed through "Romney Marsh", which I supposed was where the famous sheep breed of that name came from. And yes, there were sheep there!

The road eventually emerged from the marshland to the sea front, where miles of high concrete sea wall provided a buffer against the harsh winds and high seas for the many holiday camps, and small settlements, which were dotted along the coastline. I was intrigued too by the sight of intermittent round towers, reportedly two storey, and up to 40 feet high, and with a diameter of similar size.

At Dymchurch, a small seaside town, I was able to actually inspect one of these structures, and discovered that they were called 'Martello Towers', and were built during the Napoleonic Wars to protect the English shores from French invasion. There were five dotted along this piece of coastline in what was known as the 'Cinque Towns' (Five Ports).

Originating in Corsica in the 15th Century, they were each designed to accommodate a garrison of twenty-four men, and were strategically positioned as defence posts.

In the 19th Century, the British Empire began to build Martello Towers around the world to protect their territories. Amazingly one was built in Australia in the 1850's as protection against a Russian invasion arising out of the Crimean War which was over before the tower was finished in 1857, (Wikipedia on 'Martello Towers). This was in fact 'Fort Denison', unusually, built in the middle of Sydney Harbour, it was used to house prisoners, and is a well known landmark for all Sydneysiders.

I arrived at the incredibly busy seaport of Dover, which was set against the backdrop of the famous 'White Cliffs of Dover'. There was a dual purpose for my visit, there. Firstly, it was the point where I would leave the shores of England, to sail to France, in pursuit of the Newmarch history in Normandy. Secondly, there was family history there in Kent, which I meant to explore.

The England and Wales Census of 1881, shows that Colonel Henry Fowler Newmarch, my great, great grandfather, and his family had returned from India, and were recorded as living at "Whalmer Hall Houses, Sturry, Kent". When I first laid eyes on this Census record I was surprised to say the least, because of the number of Newmarches listed in the household. I rationalized that perhaps some of Henry's nieces and nephews were staying with the family, but I was totally shocked, that, the ten children listed, all belonged to Henry Fowler Newmarch, and upon further investigation, I discovered that my great grandfather Alfred, was actually one of twelve children!

Henry Fowler Newmarch was born on 7th February 1832 in Kurunal, West Bengal, India. On New Year's Day 1857 he married Elizabeth Barnes Sparks, the daughter of Mitchell George Sparks, in Murree Bengal, India.

They had three sons, all born in India:

Henry   (17/8/1858),

John   (10/5/1860),

Robert   (19/8/1862).

Sadly Elizabeth died 6 weeks after Robert's birth, on 6/10/1862, more than likely as a complication of her confinement.

Henry Fowler was remarried 14 months later on 14/1/1864, in Calcutta, Bengal India, to Marianne Eliza Juliana Davies, (known as Minnie), the daughter of Alfred Davies. They were prolific breeders, and produced the following large family, who appear thus in this Census:

Name	Born	Relationship	Age	Occupation	Where Born
Walter	13/2/1865	Son	16	Scholar	Bhandara India
Alfred	29/8/1867	Son	13	Scholar	{Bhandara India
Charles	1869	Son	11	Scholar	London England
George	1870	Son	10	Scholar	London England
Minnie	4/12/1872	Daughter	8	Scholar	East Indies Raipier
Oliver	1876	Son	5	Scholar	London England
Hester	1877	Daughter	4		Herne Bay Kent

| Frank | 1879 Son | 2 | London England |
| Douglas | 1880 Son | Under 6 Months | Sturry Kent England |

Poor Minnie, listed in the Census as aged 41 years, must have been pregnant for most of those seventeen years of her married life. One can't imagine what that must have been like in the heat and dust of India, especially in those days before air conditioning and refrigeration. It's no wonder that many of the children were born in the cool green climate of England.

This Census record shows Henry Fowler Newmarch as the head of the household, 49 years of age, Colonel Bengal Staff Corps, Retired, born in 'Kurunal East Indies". Also included is John Newmarch, Henry's son from his first marriage, then aged 20 years, whose occupation was listed as, "Clerk, London & County Bank".

Unsurprisingly, included in the household, are a Private Tutor, a General Servant & Cook, a House Maid, and a Nurse (Domestic).

My research failed to turn up any "Whalmer Hall Houses", which was the family's address at the time of the Census, however I did find "Whalmer Castle", so I happily took the drive north on that lovely afternoon.

I soon realized that Whalmer Castle was not the place I was looking for, but I enjoyed the experience anyway.

Whalmer Castle was built in 1539-1540 by King Henry VIII, as a fortress against French and Spanish invasion. It doesn't have a cliff-top position, as the coast there is quite flat, but it does enjoy wonderful views across the Straits of

Dover. Apparently in 1708 it became the official residence of the Lord Warden of the Cinque Ports, which were mentioned earlier. In time, the position of Lord Warden, became more of an honorary role, as the Royal Navy took charge of the defence of the British coastline.

The property is now an English Heritage property, and it is interesting to note that some of the Lords Warden have included, William Pitt the Younger, the Duke of Wellington, Sir Winston Churchill, Queen Elizabeth II, the Queen Mother, and interestingly from an Australian point of view, Sir Robert Menzies, a former long serving Australian Prime Minister.

A tour of the castle was a real history lesson, as many of the rooms contained the furniture and memorabilia of those who'd lived there. The castle had become like a country mansion for some of the Lords Warden with beautiful gardens to be admired by all. I enjoyed a sandwich at the café, which was located in the bowels of the castle, then made my way to Sturry, refocusing my attention after that pleasant diversion, on the object of my visit, Whalmer Hall Houses.

Sturry is quite close to Canterbury. It has a busy railway station, with a level crossing, which is the cause of monumental traffic jams, as the main road traffic is frequently required to stop and queue. The small village post office was my first port of call, as I imagined that they would know, more than anyone else of Whalmer Hall Houses. My enquiry drew a decidedly blank response, so I took myself over to the library, on the edge of the village green, where I garnered a similar response, and there were no local history books, which were of any benefit.

Driving around the neighbourhood, (much of the time spent in the grid lock of the level crossing debacle!), I could see that 'progress' was catching up with Sturry, and there was a lot of new development encroaching on the older historic buildings in the area. Perhaps Whalmer Hall Houses are no longer in existence? It was after all 130 years since that census was taken! Disappointed at not being able to find the last place in England where I have record of my direct ancestors, I headed back towards Dover.

However, that wasn't the end of the story! Back in Australia, I Googled 'Whalmer Hall Houses' once again, and noticed that there was a possibility that it had become a hotel, so ever hopeful, I emailed any small hotels in and around Sturry, and Canterbury which may have perhaps been the home at the centre of my enquiry. No joy!

As a last ditch attempt, I emailed Canterbury Historical Society, accidentally at first sending my enquiry to Canterbury, Connecticut, USA! Realizing my mistake, I forwarded the enquiry to Kent, England, and within an hour I received the following reply:

"Dear Wendy,

The message that you sent has been forwarded to myself at the Canterbury branch, Kent Family History Society from the Canterbury Historical Organisation in Connecticut, USA- I've not had personal contact with them (to be honest, I didn't even know there was a Canterbury in Connecticut!), but it is rather serendipitous, as I happen to live in Sturry, so am quite well placed to answer your question!

The 1881 census has a little spelling error- it should actually say

Whatmer Hall House. Could you confirm if it is the Newmarch family who are your ancestors, or a nearby entry?

If it is the former, then Whatmer Hall still stands (and indeed is the oldest building on the main road north of the village centre, having been build c.17th century, using materials from an older structure). It has been divided into two properties (Whatmer Hall and Duxbury), and look very different, even though it is one building, Whatmer having been modernised with a front verandah among other things; indeed, it would not look out of place in Australia, India, or a similar colonial setting. Duxbury is much closer to it's original appearance. There were also cottages by the main house (one of which, on the main road, grew into a large property now called Whatmer House, just to confuse matters- this house was a retirement home until recently), hence the need to know your ancestor's name to confirm I'm giving you the right information.

If you look at the website www.imagesofengland.org.uk,and register for free, you can search for the properties (type in Whatmer (or Duxbury) and Canterbury to bring them up), and you will get a photo of each, together with a bit of architectural info.

Kind regards,

David Wood, Canterbury Branch Chairman, Kent Family History Society."

What an amazing turn of events! I was so excited and grateful to David to receive this information, and again awestruck to have had my email received by David who knew so much of the history. Although I'd missed seeing the building on that trip, I now had photographs, and hope to visit it in the future.

Meanwhile back in Dover, after an incredible fortnight of discovery, which surpassed my wildest dreams, I checked in to Hubert House B&B for two nights, as my hire car would be returned the following evening, before an early morning departure the next day. I was very grateful to Peter the proprietor who lugged my bags to the top floor via the narrow winding staircase. I always seemed to be on the top floor!

Whatmer Hall Houses, Sturry Kent

Next door, was the historic "The White Horse" pub, whose gloomy interior and dark stained beams conjured up images of pirates returning from sea with their booty. However, none were present, but the walls boasted the feats of those who'd dared to swim the English Channel and conquered. Photographs of those hearty souls, and their swim times, filled the walls.

I enjoyed a good dinner but, as my diary puts it, "I didn't like the black cat wandering around the tables"!

Returning to Hubert House, I found a note on my door which read' " I'm sorry I think I've run in to your car in the B&B car park!" No! I couldn't believe it, and hurried down the three flights of stairs it inspect it. Sure enough, the rear passenger side mudguard had been scraped! As I was looking at it, a young man who was walking his rather large dog, came and introduced himself as Mark, the culprit. But I have to say a very honest culprit! He said, it shouldn't cost much to fix, then I explained that it was a rental car, and needed to be returned before 5.00pm the next day, and that there was $1,000 excess on the insurance.

It was unbelievable to think that this would happen at the last minute after two weeks of keeping the car perfect! The next morning at breakfast, I saw Mark and his young wife and baby. He was an Englishman who lived in Holland, and they were about to cross the Channel and head back to Holland that morning. He gave me his email address, and said to let him know if I could get it repaired and that he would pay for it! I thanked him for being so honest, but was unsure as to what the outcome would be.

By now, Peter, the proprietor had involved himself in the conversation, and said that he knew of someone who may be able to help. He gave me some obscure directions to the repairer who was about 15 or 20 miles out of Dover. Eventually I found the place, and Drew, the repairer. I thought I was looking at Rod Stewart! Earring, long hair, short on top, weathered and wrinkled face, and same skinny build! I explained that it was a rental car that needed to be returned by 5.00pm that afternoon. He took a long considered draw on his cigarette, scratched his chin, and said, "We might be able to do it. It'll cost you eighty pounds". Fantastic! His 'right hand man', daughter Kate, kindly dropped me at Dover Castle, which was on her way into town, and arranged to pick me up again at 3.00pm.

I spent a wonderful day there. The weather was perfect, the sun was warm and powerfully brought out the blue hues in the sky and sea, and the view was clear and fantastic over the Channel.

Dover Castle was fascinating in itself, perched on top of the white chalk cliffs, there is history of there being defences in place since A.D. 43 when the Romans invaded, but more of the castle later. What I didn't know was, was that there are over 3 miles of secret tunnels, dug into the chalky cliffs. These were first dug towards the end of the 18th Century, and housed more than 2,000 soldiers during the Napoleonic Wars. The tunnels are around 15 metres below the cliff top, and I was able to go on some exciting tours through them.

The first was the Underground Hospital tour, which lasted for 20 minutes or so, and led us through tunnels, which served as operating rooms, and emergency wards for wounded soldiers, before they could be transferred out to other facilities during World War II. We saw the limited lighting and experienced how it was when the lights went out in the middle of surgery.

Then there was the WWII Underground Tunnel Tour, which was around one hour in length and took us through the Coastal Artillery Operations room, where Admiral Sir Bertram Ramsay directed operations for the evacuation of Dunkirk against all the odds. The tour was well structured and quite involved, with plenty of Audio-visual input. It was lovely to emerge from the darkness into the sunshine on the white cliff face, overlooking the blue of the Channel, but the glare was intense!

Following a sandwich for lunch in the café, which was housed in one of the castle buildings, I went into 'the keep' and baileys, the iconic castle, which was built by King Henry II in the 12th Century. I marvelled at the skill involved in building such edifices with the limited resources that were available at that time. The view from the top of the keep was breathtaking, especially on such a beautiful day.

Kate met me as arranged, and arriving back at the workshop, I could see that the car was far from finished. Rod Stewart, AKA Drew, was deep in conversation with a buddy dreaming about moving to Brittany! I must have looked a little worried, as after 15 minutes or so, he nonchalantly turned to me and said, "Gotta wait for it to dry, can't hurry these things". I'll make you a cup of coffee, and rummaged for a 'clean' coffee mug.

He ushered me into his 'office', which was black with grease and grime, and had walls plastered with nude calendars, and somewhere under a pile of bookwork and papers was a desk. I think! I searched in vain for a clean chair after he'd invited me to sit down, and finally settled on what must have been Kate's chair, as it was the least greasy of the two. The clock ticked by, and the daydreaming for Brittany continued! Anxiously I eyed the wall clock until finally at about 4.20pm, Drew roused himself and picked up the buffer. Incredibly at 4.30pm, the car looked pristine! Drew took a rag from his overalls to dust off the white residue from the polishing, and ninety-six pounds later, (eighty pounds plus 20% VAT), was on my way. I thanked Drew immensely, who'd sure come through for me.

I arrived at the car rental office with 5 minutes to spare. The young lady came out and walked straight to the rear passenger mudguard, inspected it, then moved around the car. It was just as if she knew! Everything was fine, I breathed a sigh of relief as I headed back to Hubert House, and yes, Mark did come through with the ninety-six pounds! It went into my account just five days later. It certainly reinforces the fact that there are some good honest people in the world. Thank you Mark.

Drawbridge Entrance to Dover Castle

Chapter XVII

The P&O Ferry sailed out of Dover at 0925 hours, on yet another glorious though chilly morning, carrying a load of happy and excited passengers, some going shopping for the weekend in Paris, and some bound for the European football matches, and displaying their teams' colours in scarves, beanies, and other distinctive paraphernalia.

The white cliffs of Dover were resplendent in the morning light, capped by the magnificent Dover Castle, which stood as sentinel and protector to the coast below. The one and a half hour voyage to Calais, France on glass-like seas was soon over, and people struggled to their cars or the gangway with their quota of duty-free goods.

Local time was now 12.00 noon, and I quickly found the car rental desk, and, digging into my memory bank from almost half a century ago, pulled out some school French. It was only due to the goddess-like French Egyptian Mrs. Oran, our French teacher, who swanned into the classroom on a daily basis, that I have any memory of my school French. She was so captivating as a teacher, that Mum said I used to speak in French in my sleep!

Having successfully negotiated the car hand over, I was soon loading my already oversized luggage into a little black, diesel, Renault Twingo, which had a little more boot space than the Peugeot.

Once 'George' was switched to 'France', I set the navigator to my destination for the night, Forges-des-Eaux, in Normandy, and headed south down the motorway. It was remarkable how different everything looked, despite the fact that GB was so relatively close, and that the same sun was shining above me. For a start I was on the wrong side of the road, in a car where the gear stick and steering wheel were also on the wrong side. The architecture of barns and farmhouses was different, and when I stopped at a motorway service centre, I ate baguette avec jambon et fromage, (a ham and cheese roll), which was enormous!

After leaving the motorway, and taking the narrower more bouncy country roads, I arrived at Forges-des-Eaux at around 3.15pm, and checked in, to Le St. Denis Hotel, a small family run boutique hotel, which I'd booked on the Net. There was, the Mum, Dad, three small children, and two uncles, from what I could gather, but I didn't see any other paying guests.

The building itself was amazing, standing on a triangular corner site, it rose four storeys above the intersection, and was capped by a stylish attic façade.

The day was sparkling and there was still plenty of daylight, so I decided there was time to make the 20km trip to the village of Neufmarche, Bernard's birthplace. I passed through fields of green and gold, littered with quaint French farmhouses, before reaching the seemingly deserted village. It was strange, looking for any evidence of Bernard de Neufmarche, because everything was signposted, "Neuf-Marche", or "Neufmarche"!

I strolled round past the Mairie, or Council chambers, which was opposite a large park and community hall, thinking that there may have been some kind of monument to Bernard, but no, that appeared to be wishful thinking.

The very large, historic church, complete with a leaning slate spire and bell tower, was near the Mairie, so I crossed over to search for family history. Fortunately the giant oak door was unlocked, so I entered, and found a long narrow sanctuary, with high stonewalls colour washed in cream, and terracotta tiled floor. Instantly, it was obvious that it had been modernized, with contemporary religious paintings hanging from the high walls, the space lit by long, high gothic windows with modern leadlight patterns, in orange and blue hues, which were captured by the afternoon sunlight and exploded into the space in a riot of light and colour.

There were no pews, but rows of individual wooden chairs with wicker seats, which had a smaller wicker seat on the back of the chair, I suppose as a kneeling or resting platform for the person on the seat behind. There were six chairs on each side of the aisle, row upon row, which filled the space, probably seating around two hundred. The high arched ceiling was lined with narrow timber boards, which ran lengthwise through the church.

I moved forward to the altar area, which was through an archway, and noticed, an emblem of a knight on horseback carrying his standard, on the front of the altar table. Perhaps this was Bernard? Looking around, I was disappointed to find no other reference to Bernard in the body of the church, so left the way I had entered.

Outside in the sunshine, I noticed a freestanding

St Peter's Neuf-Marche-

building, opposite, next to the Old Presbytery, where a sandwich board attracted my attention. On closer inspection, I realized that it was a secondhand bookshop. Perhaps there was some Newmarch history in there? I soon discovered that the serious middle-aged proprietor had not a word of English. I was a little surprised at this, as it has been my experience in the past that I have struggled to compose a long sentence in French, only to find at the end, that having allowed me to stumble on in my imperfect and rusty school French, that I would be answered in perfect English, much to my embarrassment.

However, that was not the case with this patient gentleman, as I somehow asked if he had any books on local history, and told him about Bernard my ancestor. I purchased a couple of booklets, then he asked me if I had been upstairs in the church, as there was a lot of history up there!

I had noticed a staircase cut into the stonewall, in the transept, but felt that it may not be the province of strangers to venture there. I thanked him very much, then crossed the road once more and reentered the historic building.

The gentleman from the bookshop was correct. There was so much history up in that loft room, where the original old beams were exposed, and historic documents and photos were arranged around the walls. The story on the walls told that this church was originally a Benedictine Monastery, and there were photographs of the ruins of the Chateau of Neufmarche, where Bernard was born, and, in French, reference to his father Geoffrey, and his Viking grandfather

Turquetil.

There was information about Bernard, and his exploits in accompanying William the Conqueror in victory over the English in A.D.1066, as well as Bernard's brother 'Drogon', who entered the abbey of Saint-Evroult, which apparently was associated with Saint Benedict. One article made the point that, one brother a soldier, one a priest, established a tradition.

As I was taking photographs, and trying to translate and comprehend the wealth of history, which surrounded me, I suddenly heard the clang of bolts and locks, which reverberated across the hard lifeless, surfaces, and had a sudden panic, that I was being locked in!

I hurried downstairs, but rationalized that there was a doorway out to the priory. Big black bolts across the oak front door, signalled, that yes, it had been locked! I rushed to the door, which led from the transept, but no! It had no handle! Now I was really panicking, and had visions of having to sleep the night in there, and it was already becoming quite cool. Realizing that there was no other way out other than the tightly bolted front door, I let out a couple of very loud, "Hello"s, feeling that it was a vain attempt, as I looked skyward to the high, unreachable windows.

Mercifully I heard the locks clanging on the front door, and a small shocked sister in a grey habit and black jacket materialized, her eyes like saucers, at the sight of her unintended captive, me! (I now know her name is Sister Marie-Archange, or Archangel). She certainly was an angel sent to rescue me! We had a garbled exchange in French, as we embraced and kissed, and both felt unbelievable relief. She was apologizing profusely, and I was telling her that I thought that I was going to be spending the night there! It was so close to being a reality, as her car was parked about two metres from the front door, ready to drive away!

Thank you Lord, is all I could say, as I crossed the road once more to thank the monsieur in the bookshop for the information about the history in the loft, although inwardly I was unnerved, at how close I had come to a cold dark night!

Back at Forges-des-Eaux, I had time to take in some of the beautiful French architecture before dinner. The Hotel de Ville, or town hall was amazing. Entering through the carriageway, next to a five storey clock tower, one emerges to park like surroundings, and buildings with ornate brickwork, some with exposed oak frames, high pitched, curved slate roofs, black wrought iron lamplights, gabled dormer windows in the lofts, leadlight windows, elaborate chimneys, and all manner of beautiful features. The well, a reminder of bygone days was present there in the courtyard.

The rear of the buildings, which could be seen in the courtyard, were much more ornate than the exterior wall, that faced the roadway. I believe that this was done so as to make the exterior of the buildings less appealing to thieves, who may have believed that, the less the embellishment, the less the riches to steal inside, and so deter them.

Madame at Le St Denis, served me, Le Menu, which consisted of, little olives and hors d'oevres, green salad, grilled pork with ratatouille and frittes (chips). Then for

The Little Sister who Rescued Me.

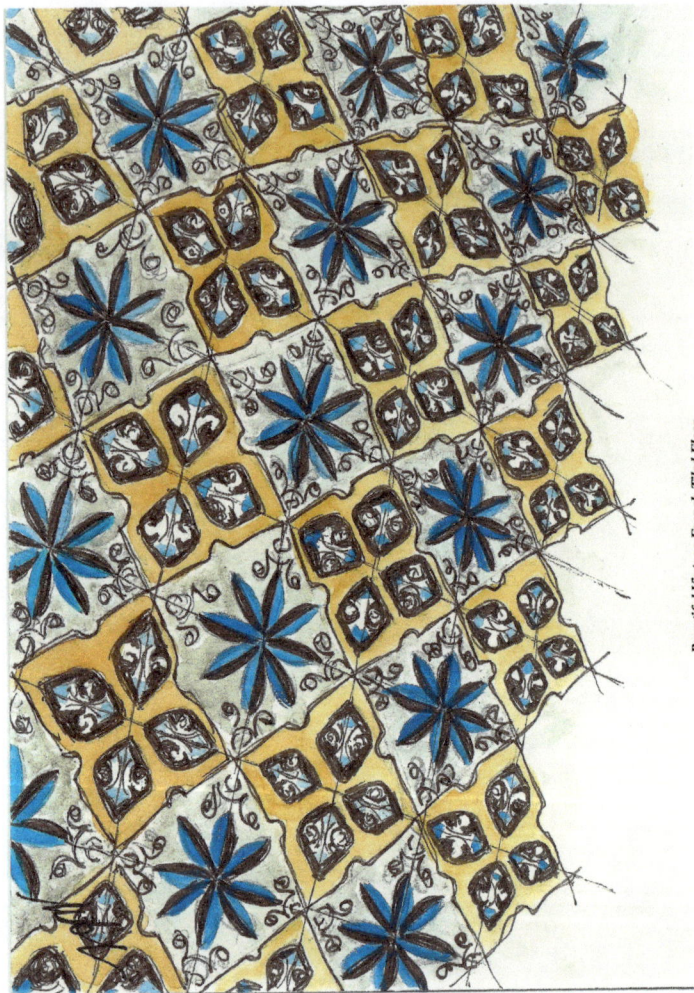

Beautiful Vintage French Tiled Floor

Beautiful French Architecture featuring Oak Framing & red clay Bricks

197

Example of Ornate French Brickwork

dessert, delectable crème caramel. All in all, a delicious French meal, served in the cosy dining room, where low dark oak beams and French antiques were a feature, along with a beautiful old floor, of blue patterned tiles.

Chapter XVIII

Croissants and a bowl of hot chocolate next morning was followed by fond farewells to Madam and Monsieur, and a visit to the small Farmers' Market which was setting up in a cul-de-sac across the road.

It wasn't large, but it was interesting, with anything from fresh poultry, rabbits, cheeses, wine and fresh veggies, to a weaver with wicker and cane, ready to repair wicker seats, such as I'd seen in the church at Neufmarche.

I set my course for Bayeux, which was about three hours east of Forges-des-Eaux, and quite close to the Normandy Coast. En route, I drove into Buchy, a beautiful little medieval market town, which still had its ancient covered marketplaces, where hanging baskets of vivid red geraniums, contrasted with the weathered oak frame work, and slate roofs. The Mairie sat pompously between the two covered marketplaces, its tall bell tower dominating, as if to command respect.

Patisseries displayed shelf after shelf of mouth-watering cakes and pastries of every description, and the aroma of garlic infused charcoal chicken, turning on the footpath rotisserie, wafted on the cold morning air.

I pushed on to Bayeux, where a system of one way streets, took me around in circles, via a central park, which was surrounded by shopping streets. I arrived at my destination, Le Monastere Sainte Trinite, a Benedictine Monastery, which was difficult to find, down another one-way street. 'George', my navigator, announced that I had arrived at my destination, so I found a rare parking spot in the narrow street, opposite No. 48. All that was visible, in this seemingly residential street, was a high grey fence, with an iron gate giving access to a flight of five or six steps, at the top of which the path led through the garden to a tall, open entry door.

I stepped in to the high vaulted foyer, with a mosaic tile floor, and a glass window to the right. As my eyes adjusted to the dim light, I noticed, behind the glass, a very small, very old, nun in her habit, slumped forward, completely double, and sound asleep in a cane chair padded with cushions! She was obviously the guard!

I deliberated for a few minutes as to what to do, fearing that a sudden shock may kill her! Eventually, I opened the window, and said, "Bonjour ma Soeur". Yes, I did startle her! She struggled to life, mumbling, 'oo la las', and when she succeeded in prising herself from the chair, she was still completely doubled over, and barely reached the height of the windowsill! She was very deaf, so between my French, and her inability to hear me, we didn't make much ground. She instructed me to sit on the wooden form behind me, before shuffling off, still doubled over, her frantic, feeble calls for assistance fading from earshot as she went. Eventually she returned, shuffling back and settling into her cane chair, meanwhile I remained for some fifteen minutes on the wooden form as instructed, feeling very much that I'd arrived at Maria's abbey, from 'The Sound of Music'.

The high gothic doors at the end of the foyer, which led to the cloister, finally opened to reveal a much younger,

Sister Marie-Pierre, who welcomed me warmly, and told me that my room wouldn't be ready until 4.00pm.

The Monastery was centrally located, so I left the car parked where it was, and walked to see 'The Bayeux Tapestry', which is housed in a beautiful former villa, now known as "Musee de la Tapesserie de Bayeux", which is not far from the Bayeux Cathedral, or the Cathedrale Notre Dame de Bayeux.

Entering the villa through a covered carriageway on cobblestones, the image of the three sided, four storey building was breathtaking. A traditional Viking boat, built with the same techniques, as were employed in the 10th and 11th centuries, took pride of place in the courtyard.

To view the "Tapestry", one enters a darkened, climate-controlled area, where, in a continuous curved glass case, and following the flow of the three-sided building, the incredibly detailed Bayeux Tapestry is displayed. A hand held Audio guide, explained the fifty scenes, pointing out individuals in the scenes, and refreshing the story I'd heard at Battle.

The Bayeux Tapestry is an amazing piece of art and history, whose colours have remained strong for almost a thousand years. It is 70 metres or 230 feet long, and 50cm or 20 inches high, and the embroidered work of coloured wool on a linen strip, is a graphic representation of the Norman Invasion, and the Battle of Hastings, including the preamble, when Edward the Confessor, King of England, sent Harold to France to tell William that he was chosen as Edward's successor to the English throne. The tapestry also

The Front Entrance of Le Monastere Sainte Trinitere Bayeux

depicts Harold swearing allegiance to William before double crossing him, and being crowned King of England instead, which then led to the invasion of A.D. 1066.

William's half brother Bishop Odo, was the Bishop of Bayeux, and features prominently in the tapestry, and it is believed that he commissioned the work in about A.D. 1070, and had it made in Kent, England, where he had a strong power base. This theory is supported by the Latin text used on the work, which has Anglo-Saxon connotations.

One theory has it that the tapestry was commissioned by Queen Matilda, William's wife, and that it was produced by her ladies in waiting. However, this is not considered to have much credence.

The Tapestry, which is not a tapestry, as such, but an intricate piece of embroidery, was found in the nearby Bayeux Cathedral, where Bishop Odo was the Bishop, and in fact began the building of the cathedral in A.D. 1070. The Bayeux Tapestry was displayed annually in the cathedral, as a way of telling the history of the invasion and the related politics, to the illiterate population at the time.

I emerged into the now weakening sunlight, and crossed the narrow ancient street, to a very cute outdoor café, at the site of a watermill, where I enjoyed a café crème, before wandering back to the monastery, soaking in the atmosphere of the beautiful old French architecture, full of style and charm.

My wait this time was brief. I was greeted warmly in French, by the same tiny doubled over Sister, who had now woken and come to life, and in fact was very animated,

Home of the Bayeux Tapestry

and apologizing profusely, as it seems, in her almost comatosed state, she had been confused as to the reason for my visit!

Sister Marie-Pierre appeared briefly, and handed me on to Sister Cecile, the deputy hospitality manager, who was also young. She was very bright and bubbly, with dancing eyes, a contrast to her long black habit and white wimple, and certainly didn't look to be the 37years of age, which I later learned that she was, and that she had been at the monastery for thirteen years! She told me that the old Sister, who was now giving me lots of hugs and kisses, was one of two nuns there who were 94years old, and that her name was Sister Joan of Arc, which Sister Cecile was in awe of!

It transpires that this Benedictine Monastery, (Monastere de la Trinite), owes its existence to Queen Matilda, wife of William the Conqueror, King William I of England, who, on June 18th, 1066 just months prior to the Norman Conquest, was present with her husband, the then, William, Duke of Normandy, with their children at the consecration of the Holy Trinity Abbey, in Caen. Perhaps in a bid to gain Divine blessing, as well as the blessing of the church for the battle that he was soon to embark on, Annie Fettu, in her book, "Queen Matilda", reveals that William took his daughter Cecily by the hand and led her to the altar where she was offered to the abbey, of which William's cousin Matilda, was the first abbess.

This prompted others to offer their daughters, and even their mothers, to the abbey, and rich endowments were given to the church. Matilda took an active role in the work of the abbeys, and along with her kind deeds, was a generous benefactor to the church. It seems that she donated money to restore the refectory in St, Evroult, which was the Order that Bernard's brother Drogon, joined, as mentioned in Chapter 17. In 1648, three sisters from the Holy Trinity Abbey in Caen, travelled to Bayeux, and established this very monastery.

Sister Cecile then took me on a tour of the sections of the monastery which were not private, and furnished me with a key for entry to the car park. Sister Marie Pierre was busy seeing off a group of girl guides who had apparently spent the weekend camping in the grounds. The Monastery was made up of three buildings that formed a U-shape, and were linked by the cloister, which overlooked the large grassed courtyard, that filled the inside of the 'U'.

The buildings on each side of the 'U', were matching three storey plus attic, stone and slate buildings, with impressive archways along the ground floors, and tall windows with Juliet balconies, on the second and third floors, and skylight windows in the slate roofed attics. One of these buildings housed the kitchen and dining rooms, (including the guest dining room), on the ground floor, and the Sisters sleeping and living quarters on the top two floors. The other building had some offices, conference room, and library on the ground floor, and the upper two floors were accommodation floors for guests.

The end of the 'U' was St Michael's Chapel, where the Sisters offered prayers every three hours.

In the Cloisters of Bayeux Monastery

The Author with Sister Cecile in the Dining Room

My room was painted baby blue and was newly refurbished, very comfortable, and contained a cubicle ensuited bathroom, faux timber flooring, a combination wardrobe/dressing table, desk and bed. The high casement windows opened in, revealing the beautifully ornate wrought iron panel with timber handrail, of the Juliet balcony, which overlooked the courtyard and the twin building opposite, where our dining room was situated.

I decided to go to prayers at 7.30pm before dinner. As I waited outside the Chapel in the cloister for the bell to ring, Sister Joan of Arc came along, her posture, so bowed, that she didn't see me until she was within a metre of me. For the second time that day, I feared that I may be the cause of her having a heart attack! As she was almost upon me, she let out a shocked grunt, adjusted her gait, and kept walking!

Sister Cecile told me that that there was another sister in that community, who was a few months younger than Sister Joan of Arc, but that she'd been there longer, having joined the Monastery during the Second World War.

I entered the large, dark chapel, and through the gloom could see many stone statues, and stained glass windows, unusually without picture stories, but containing coloured diamond shaped glass panels.

Eight Sisters entered, one or two hurrying in a little late. The prayers were all sung, and were led by Sister Marie Pierre who played a small table instrument, which sounded like a harpsichord. Apparently it was of Austrian origin but Sister Marie Pierre called it a Sitar, which surprised me, as I'd only ever heard of the Indian Sitar.

The music was hauntingly beautiful and harmonious. I mostly just listened, as it was in French anyway. When it was over, the Sisters left in silence, and the two of us who shared in the prayers, went to dinner. Besides me, there was a tall Frenchman with a beard, and no moustache, and glasses. I had been introduced to him earlier as Jean-Pierre, a 'locum' priest from Paris.

We crossed the rather unkempt courtyard, and entered the huge dining room, with amazingly high ceilings, and a beautiful, old mosaic tiled floor. Carved antique dressers filled the wall spaces in between the regular openings of the high windows and doors.

Just one table was set with eight places, and six older men stood chatting in the enormous space. Surprise, surprise, Sister Cecile, who must have run from the Chapel, came through the door, which led from the kitchen, pushing a large hot box into the room, before greeting us and departing the way she came.

One of the men gave thanks, and the priest from Paris who had joined me in the Chapel, informed me in French, "You are with seven priests"! Apparently, these six men were friends of the man who had recently become the Bishop of Bayeux, and he'd invited his old friends to come see his cathedral!

Following the blessing, we enjoyed a true French feast. The entrée of devilled eggs on lettuce was already on a platter on the table, and that was passed around. There were copious amounts of bread, as one of the priests rose to cut the long baguette, only one slice at a time each, in case it went stale!

From the hot box came;

- Poached fish in white herb sauce and zucchini bake.

More bread, followed by a wonderful cheese platter, which included brie, and camembert.

Dessert was delicious creamy rice, all washed down by Jugs of water and Bayeux Apple Cider, made by the monks at a nearby monastery!

There was a lovely spirit of sharing as the food was passed around, amongst us. At the conclusion of the meal, we washed up, and set the table for breakfast just as Sister Marie Pierre appeared to bid us good night, as it was then around 9.00pm and she had just led the prayers again.

At the time of my visit, this Monastery had only ten sisters, and most of them were elderly, very elderly. The Reverend Mother was sick at the time, and apparently had been for some time, so the burden of most of the work seemed to fall on the two younger sisters, Marie Pierre, and Cecile, which did make me wonder about the sustainability of such a situation.

Next morning after breakfast, I walked to the nearby cathedral, which was huge and elaborate, and I bumped into some of my fellow lodger priests. It was on that very site, where the Bayeux Cathedral stands, that Harold Godwinson swore an oath of allegiance to William Duke of Normandy, the breaking of which led to the English Invasion and the Battle of Hastings.

During my visit to Bayeux, I took the opportunity to

Inside Bayeux Cathedral

Rear View of Bayeux Catedral

visit some of the coastal towns and ports, one of which was Granville, which is actually quite close to the Channel Islands of Jersey and Guernsey. The ninety minute drive took me down tiny lanes, past the maize harvest, through forests and small villages. The countryside was a picture of vibrant green.

The tide was out – a long way, almost as if the plug had been taken out of the bathtub. The sun was shining on the cold blue distant waves, as I sat in an outdoor café to have coffee. One crazy person was swimming!

I arrived back just in time for Vespers, and enjoyed the Sisters' sweet singing of the prayers. Earlier in the day I visited the Sisters' Shop, which sold souvenirs, postcards, Monastic chocolate, the Brothers' cider, and books. The sister who was working there was very persuasive, but I managed to emerge with only a few souvenirs just before she had to run off for midday prayers called, Sext.

I wondered how the Sisters managed to get any work done at all, in between their hectic daily prayer schedule. The six sets of prayers, each lasting 15 – 20 minutes, which were announced by the ringing of the Monastery bell, (I can just see Sister Cecile flying on those bell ropes), went like this:

- Lauds   07.00
- Mass/Terce 0830
- Sext   12 Midday
- Vespers   17.30
- Compline   19.00 (Approximately)
- Vigil   20.45

We enjoyed another delicious dinner. The six priests who were friends of the Bishop, were visiting him for dinner that night, but Jean-Pierre, and two other ladies were present, and we enjoyed:

- Entrée   Pink grapefruit
- Main   Delicious steak and tomato
  Carrots and peas
- Dessert   Cheese platter,
  Fresh pineapple (very sweet & juicy)
- Apple cider (4.8%)! Jugs of water
- Copious amounts of delicious baguette.

Next morning I drove to Arromanches, which is the closest beach to Bayeux, and the one of the beaches involved in the D-Day landings of World War II. Plenty of evidence of that time remains with landing bridges and concrete blocks used in the landing, still in the water. The waterfront was littered with tourist coaches, disgorging their passengers, (many of them American), into the museum, and onto the beaches. The houses along the beachfront were large and beautiful, many of them boarded up for the approaching winter. The cold winds gave me a reason to wear my duffle coat, which I enjoyed immensely. On top of a cliff stood an iconic chateau with conical towers, and I wondered how it had survived the bombardment of war.

I continued on along the coast, passing fields where mountains of harvested turnips were piled high in the ploughed field. Everywhere there were apples, apples and more apples. The trees were laden, and windfalls littered the ground they stood on.

I moved on to the beautiful seaside fishing village of Hornfleur, famous for its character and history, where a wall of narrow six and seven storey buildings rises from the waterfront promenade, and old wooden sailing boats with coloured sails, and fishing vessels, conger up images of romance and adventure. I walked through the narrow cobbled streets, enjoying the atmosphere, as have so many artists and writers through the centuries.

I stepped into a narrow fronted café, where the light was dim, which added to its ambiance. I was delighted to meet two young Australians there, and we shared travel stories right through afternoon tea, and I enjoyed delicious home made apple tart and coffee.

Chapter XIX

Next morning I bade farewell to the priests, Sister Cecile, and Bayeux, and headed to Falaise, the birthplace of William the Conqueror.

The morning was cold as the tyres of the little black Renault Twingo rumbled across the cobblestones and up the hill to the chateau, and having parked the car I walked up to the entrance, where to my utter dismay I read the piece of paper, which was stuck over the entry sign, and in French said, "Unusually today the Chateau is closed"! Nooooo! I couldn't believe what I was seeing!

The cold morning contributed to me needing to answer a call of nature. Still smarting over the chateau being closed, I decided to ask the receptionist at the adjacent Mairie, or Council Chambers, if I could use their toilet. She directed me down a long narrow passageway. As I was coming back, I looked up, and noticed an enormous, very impressive ornate bronze wall mount, which was probably about 2.5 – 3 metres high, and about 2 metres wide.

As I translated the French in my head, I could barely believe what I was reading. The translation read: "The Companions of William, 1st Duke of Normandy at Hastings MLXVI (1066)". Then below were listed approximately two hundred and forty names of those companions. I quickly scanned the list, and yes, Bernard de Neufmarche was there on the list! It was difficult to conceal my excitement, and I marvelled yet again at the bizarre

My First Glimpse of William the Conqueror's Chateau

Entry Point to William the Conqueror's Chateau

List of the Companions of William the Conqueror in the Mairie

221

Bernard de Neufmarche's name on the List of the Companions of William the Conqueror as Seen in the Mairie at Falaise

string of events, which had led me to be in the Mairie at all to see this extraordinary site.

I wandered around the interesting shopping streets of Falaise, before succumbing to a lovely family owned restaurant, La Renaissance Café, which seemed to be popular with the locals for lunch.

Plat de jour was: Thick ham with potato bake, and delicious mustard sauce, followed by scrumptious homemade pineapple tart. MMM!

The whole of the commercial world shuts down between 12midday, and 2.30pm, even the supermarket and service stations, which is unthinkable to the Australian psyche. One wonders how anybody makes a living!

I motored on via the lovely, and quite trendy town of Alencon, which is famous for its lace, to La Chapelle Montligeon, my destination for the next two nights. The route became more and more narrow, as I wound my way though hedgerows and grazing land, and I wondered if George was leading me astray! Suddenly, as I reached the crest of a hill, in the distance, at least a kilometre or two away, there on the side of a hill were enormous, palatial buildings. Could that really be where I would spend the next two nights?

The laneway took me down the hill, across a small bridge which was decorated with colourful flower baskets, and up through the very pretty old village, past the massive basilica, to the entrance of the monastery and hermitage.

Arriving at reception, which was located in a huge 'lobby' area, was akin to arriving at a five star hotel, where

Reception staff, at a proper Reception Desk, greeted me. I laughed to myself, remembering the very different welcome I received at Monastere Sainte Trinite La Joie Saint Benoit, at Bayeux. La Chapelle Montligeon, obviously boasts a much larger budget, than the Sisters have at Bayeux, where poor Sister Marie Pierre, and Sister Cecile, are run off their feet, and have to resort to putting the ninety-four year old Sister Joan of Arc, on the door!

La Chapelle Montligeon, was built by Father Paul Buguet at the end of the 19th Century, when he was the village priest. Following the sudden deaths of his brother and two nieces, he began praying for the souls of the departed, and that became the focus of the Order of priests and sisters there. Thousands of pilgrims, apparently make the journey to La Chapelle Montligeon each year, to pray for the souls of their dear departed loved ones, and in fact retreats, and teaching seminars are run there throughout the year, which is obviously a source of income, along with bequests and donations from family members.

The order of Sisters there appears to comprise younger women, who wear white habits, and are not afraid to show other clothing underneath, or to complement their habits with coloured scarves. I believe that they live in the village, and I did see two of their number wiz past me in an old car!

My room in the hermitage wasn't large, but I had the most marvellous view out over the enormous formal rose gardens and central fountain, to the rural landscape beyond.

View from my Window at the Hermitage

At dinner, which was served to us by waitstaff, I met several 'pilgrims', an elderly French lady who was accompanied by her son and daughter-in-law. They had come to pray for the soul of her deceased husband. There were also several elderly people who I believe live in the hermitage.

Next morning, following 'a French Breakfast' of bread, butter and jam, which is liberally dunked in a large bowl of milk coffee, I decided to head back to Falaise once again, however, at 9.20am, the temperature outside was minus one degree Celsius, and the windscreen of the car was encrusted with a thick white layer of ice!

Eventually I was able to clear the windscreen, and I drove off into a clear blue, albeit cold day, and headed once more for William the Conqueror's chateau at Falaise.

In the end I found it a little disappointing, because imposing as it was, it's restorers had modernized it and brought it into the 21st Century, which I felt diminished it's authenticity greatly.

Back at La Chapelle Montligeon, I was shown a DVD about the history of the Basilica, and the work of the Order, which the 'powers that be', insist on everyone seeing. I had time for a relaxing stroll around the sweet village, before attending Vespers in the Basilica at 18.45 hours. The nine or ten white habited Sisters sang beautifully in harmony, and the resident Frenchman, who I'd met in the dining room, (I believe that he may be a retired priest), sang very loudly! For the Sisters, this was their last public prayers for the day, a much lighter load than the Sisters at Bayeux.

That night the dining room was full. As well as those present the evening before, there were another twenty-two people who were there for a seminar, as well as another couple who were spending the night. The three older residents seemed a little institutionalized, as they ferreted for their favourite flavoured yoghurt and jams, leaving the visitors to take the leftovers!

The next morning, as I was checking out, a young priest who spoke English, was appointed to me to give me the "hard sell", about donating to the Basilica, and their work. He plied me with lots of literature, and asked me to pass it on to others in Australia. Unfortunately, as an Evangelical Christian, I believe that its too late when you're dead to try to gain Salvation, but that its only by accepting God's free gift of Salvation while you are alive on this earth, that you can gain entry into Heaven, by God's grace.

The morning was minus two degrees, cold and frosty once again, on this my last day in France, as I drove into the clear blue morning, the sun valiantly rising to bring warmth to the earth.

I calculated that on my way to Paris, I had time to visit Giverny to see the house and garden of Claude Monet, the famous Impressionist painter. What a delight it was, to wander down Rue de Claude Monet, or (Claude Monet Street), which is the destination, not just his house and garden.

The house, which is engulfed by the garden, is an elongated two storey stone house featuring green window shutters and woodwork. My favourite room was the bright

Monet's Beautiful House at Giverney

yellow kitchen, with yellow furniture, and blue and white wall tiles, above the enormous wood-burning stove. The garden was a picture of cottage plants, which were so colourful and vibrant, despite the fact that it was almost two months through autumn. At the bottom of the garden, was the iconic waterlily pond, and Japanese bridge, which featured in some of Monet's paintings, along with the punt, also iconic in his paintings, which was pulled up against the bank. On that beautiful sunny day, it was easy to see where Monet's inspiration came from.

Eventually, I realized I had a train to catch, so pointed the car in the direction of Paris, and enjoyed the drive, which followed the River Seine, but became more and more congested as I approached peak hour in gay Paris.

George took me up the Champs-Elysees to the Arc de Triomphe, which I reached at 4.00pm on that Friday afternoon, where the roundabout at the top was solid with traffic. Manic was not the word for it! I made it through the mayhem, George instructing me to take the sixth exit, which turned out to be straight down the other side. From there it took me a full forty-five minutes in a traffic crawl to travel the short distance to Gare de Lyon, where I would hand back the hire car. As I edged along in the absolute snail pace traffic, motor bikes sped by, only millimeters from my car's shiny duco! Firmly fixed in my mind, was the last minute miss hap with my last shiny black car in Dover, so I prayed fervently to be saved from any more dramas of that kind.

I arrived at the car return with just fifteen minutes to spare, and unscathed, which I was very grateful for. Due to a string of events which I won't bore or stress the reader with, I arrived with only minutes to spare to catch my 7.00pm overnight train to Rome, leaving no time for any food since my sandwich at lunchtime, so I determined to enjoy a good meal aboard the train. As I struggled aboard with my accumulated luggage, I was handed a five-hundred millilitre bottle of water by a station official, which I thought was nice, but unusual.

My fellow passengers were a group of French artists, who were heading off on a painting trip to Florence. As we settled in to conversation, they told me that due to an industrial strike, there was no dining car on the train, which is why we had been handed a small bottle of water, our sole ration until 11.00am the next day!

I was blest once again, as my newly acquired travelling companions, lavishly shared their baguette, sheep cheese, and jambon, (ham), with me as we chugged our way through the Alps into Italy, which brought to a close a chapter in this wonderful adventure of the Quest to follow the Newmarches through history.

Acknowledgements

This book would not have happened, had it not been for the work of Charles Henry Newmarch, and Frederick George Newmarch, in writing The Newmarch Pedigree, which was my roadmap for this 'quest'.

The pages of this work are full of stories of those who helped me on my way and pointed me in the right direction, and as such this story is about them as much as the history, and I thank them for their contributions.

I am indebted to family and friends who have encouraged me along the way. For my son Matthew and my niece Lisa who read the draft text and gave me feedback and encouragement.

I am especially grateful to Lisa for her genius as a graphic artist, and her technical support and help with typesetting, and the finer points of pre publishing.

Bibliography

Allen, Charles, *Tales from the Raj.* London: Abacus, 2010.

Bailey, Catherine, *Black Diamonds: The Rise and Fall of an English Dynasty.* London: Penguin, 2008.

Barber, Nicola and Andy Langley, *Children's British History Encyclopedia: Discover the Remarkable Story of Britain's Past,* Bath: Parragon, 2008.

Barish, Eileen, *Lodging in Britain's Monasteries.* Scottsdale, Arizona: Anacapa, 2009.

Barish, Eileen, *Lodging in France's Monasteries.* Scottsdale, Arizona: Anacapa, 2006.

Bates, David, *William the Conqueror.* Stroud, Gloucestershire: Tempus, 2004.

Bryant, Geoffrey F., *The Church of St. Lawrence, Thornton Curtis: A Short History and Guide.* Barton-on-Humber, The Church of St. Lawrence, Thornton Curtis, 1987.

Bryson, Bill, *At Home: A Short History of Private Life.* London: Transworld, 2010.

Bartholomew Mapping, *2002 Collins Road Atlas: Britain.* London: Collins, 2001.

Bartholomew Mapping, *2003 Collins Road Atlas: Europe.* London: Collins, 2003.

Coad, Jonathan, *Battle Abbey and Battlefield.* London: English Heritage, 2010.

Cooper, J.P. (Ed. for the Royal Historical Society), *Wentworth Papers 1597-1628: Camden Fourth Series, Volume 12.* London: University College, 1973.

Daniell, Christopher, *Death & Burial in Medieval England 1066 - 1550.* London: Routledge, 1998.

David, Saul, *The Indian Mutiny.* London: Penguin, 2003.

Erskine, Barbara, *Lady of Hay: Fascinating, Absorbing and Original.* London: Sphere Books, 1987.

Fettu, Annie, *Queen Matilda: Princess of Flanders: Duchess of Normandy: Queen of England: Circa 1032-1083.* Cully, France: Orep Editions, 2005.

Fettu, Annie, *William the Conqueror: Born out of Wedlock in Falaise: Duke of Normandy: King of England: 1027-1087.* Cully, France: Orep Editions, 2009.

Fox-Davies, Arthur Charles, *Heraldry Explained.* London: T.C. & E. C. Jack, Circa 1905.

Heighway, Caroline, Susan Hamilton, David Hoyle, Frances Kay, Robin Lunn, and Celia Thomson, *Gloucester Cathedral: Faith Art and Architecture: 1000 Years.* London: Scala Publishers, 2011.

Heuillard, Jacques, *Neuf-Marche Autrefois. Societe Historique et Geographique du Bassin de l'Epte,* Les Cahiers de la S.H.G.B.E. Nos. 19-20 1987-1988

Jones, Huw (Original Text), Smith, R.J.L., (Ed)., *Brecon Cathedral, (Fourth Edition).* Shropshire: RJL Smith & Assoc. Much Wenlock for Friends of Brecon Cathedral, 2008.

Le Cato Edwards, W., *Epworth: The Home of the Wesleys.* (No details of publication available).

McMillan, Margaret, *Women of the Raj: The Mothers, Wives, and Daughters of the British Empire in India.* New York: Random House Trade Paperbacks, 2007.

Morris, Richard, K., *Kenilworth Castle*. London: English
    Heritage, 2010.

Newmarch, Charles Henry, *Five years in the East*. Reprints
    from the Collection of the University of Michigan
    Library, 2011.

Newmarch, Charles Henry, *Five Years in the East, Volume 2.*
    Reprinted from the Collection of the University of
    California, Berkely Library, 2011.

Newmarch, Geo. Fred., and Chas. H., *The Newmarch
    Pedigree: Verified by Public Records, Authentic
    Manuscripts, and General and Local Histories: Printed
    for Private Circulation Only*. Cirencester, 1868.

North Yorkshire Shire Council, *The Wood hall Moated Manor
    Project*. Knottingly, North Yorkshire: The Wood Hall
    Moated Manor Project, 1995.

Royal Commission on the Ancient and Historical Monuments
    of Wales, The Dean and Chapter of Brecon Cathedral,
    *The cathedral Church of St John the Evangelist Brecon:
    An Architectural Study*. Mid Glamorgan, Wales: The
    Friends of Brecon Cathedral, 1994.

Steward, Rob, and Kenilworth History & Archaelogical
    Society (KHAS), *A Guide to the Historic Town of
    Kenilworth*. Kenilworth: The Pleasaunce Press for KHAS
    and Kenilworth Town Council, 2003.

Webster Appleton, Avril E, *Looking Back at Micklegate:
    Nunnery Lane & Bishophill: York*. York: Reeder
    Publications, 2011.

Articles

ancestry.com Searches:

Charles Newmarch, 14/02/2011.

Elizabeth Newmarch, 22/01/2012.

George Newmarch, 21/02/2011.

Henry Newmarch, 6/02/2012.

John Newmarch, 24/08/2011.

William Newmarch, 22/01/2012.

1851 England Census for Henry Newmarch, 17/03/2012.

1861 England Census for Henry Newmarch, 17/03/2012.

1861 England Census for Violet Newmarch, 17/03/2012.

1881 England Census:

>*Henry Fowler Newmarch,*
>
>*Minnie Newmarch,*
>
>*John Newmarch,*
>
>*Walter Newmarch,*
>
>*Alfred Newmarch,*
>
>*Charles Newmarch,*
>
>*George Newmarch,*
>
>*Minnie Newmarch,*
>
>*Oliver Newmarch,*
>
>*Hester Newmarch,*
>
>*Frank Newmarch,*
>
>*Douglas Newmarch, 6/02/2011.*

1901 England Census for Charles Newmarch, 11/02/2011.

Australia Birth Index, 1788-1922:

>*Richmond H. Chapman, 10/02/2011.*

Australia Marriage Index, 1788-1949:

Richmond H. Chapman/Harriet C.G. Newmarch,
10/02/2011.

Australian Electoral Rolls, 1903-1954:

1930: Catherine Newmarch, 29/08/2011.

1936: Richmond Hull Chapman, 10/02/2011.

1937: Richmond Hull Chapman, 10/02/2011.

1949: Richmond Hull Chapman, 10/02/2011.

England & Wales Marriages, 1538-1940:

Thomas Fowler to Ann Newmarch, 18/02/2011.

New South Wales, Australia, Unassisted Immigrant Passenger Lists, 1826-1922:

A Newmarch, (1885),

F.R. Newmarch, (1907),

Mrs Newmarch, (1884),

Mr. Newmarch, (1884),

Dr. Newmarch, (1886),

Mr. Newmarch, (1886),

Messier Newmarch, (1888),

Mrs Newmarch, (1888),

Dr. Newmarch, (1889),

Miss Newmarch, (1898),

Master Newmarch, (1899), Newmarch, (1887),

Geo. Newmarch, (1892),

Mr. L.A. Newmarch, (1883),

Mr. L W Newmarch, (1889),

T. Newmarch, (1898),

Capt. Newmarch, (1901),

Mr. Newmarch, (1901),

A.S. Newmarch, (1901), 11/02/2011.

Chas. Newmarch, (1886), 11/02/2012.

Roots Web (An Ancestry.com community).

"The Golden Falcon", Chapter VII/4 - 'Redrose',
Yorkist heirs, 16/05/2012.

ancestry.com.au Searches

All Australian Birth Index, 1788-1922:
Newmarch, 10/02/2011.

Australian Death Index, 1787-1985:
Richmond Barry Chapman, 10/02/2011.
Harriet Mary Newmarch, 26/08/2011.

All Australian Electoral Rolls, 1903-1954:
Alfred Newmarch, 5/02/2011.

Australian Marriage Index:
Alfred Newmarch, 26/08/2011.
Alice Mary Newmarch, 26/08/2011.
Harriet C G Newmarch, 26/08/2011.
Violet M Newmarch, 26/08/2011.
Walter Newmarch, 26/08/2011.

Sands Directories: Sydney and New South Wales, Australia,
1858-1933:
Alfred Newmarch: 1892, 26/08/2011.
Alfred Newmarch: 1897, 26/08/2011.
Alfred Newmarch: 1905, 26/08/2011.
Alfred Newmarch: 1908, 26/08/2011.
Alfred Newmarch: 1913, 26/08/2011.
Rev. Walter Newmarch: 1907, 29/08/2011.

All Sands Directories: Sydney and New South Wales,
Australia, 1858-1933:
Walter Newmarch, 29/08/2011.

1871 England Census :

> *Violet Newmarch,* 18/03/2012.

England & Wales, FreeBDM Death Index: 1837-1915

> *Violet Newmarch, (1875),* 17/03/2012.

England & Wales, National Probate Calendar (Index of Wills and Administrations*), 1861-1941:*

> *Violet Newmarch,* 17/03/2012.

ancestry.co.uk Searches

Henry Newmarch,   29/01/2012.

> *Oxford University Alumni, 1500-1886.*

Overviews:

> *Edward Newmarch, Born (01/ 1674),* 27/01/2012.
>
> *John March Newmarch, Born (24/ 12/ 1646),* 21/09/2011.
>
> *John March Newmarch, Born (12/ 02/ 1672),* 21/09/2011.
>
> *Joseph Newmarch, Born (10/ 08/ 1747),* 22/01/2012.
>
> *Robert March Newmarch, Born (About 1621),* 27/01/2012.
>
> *William Newmarch, Born (6/ 06/ 1710),* 22/01/2012.

Family Group Sheet:

> *Halstead/ Newmarch/ Barnes Family tree*

British Library India Office Family History Search

> *Jane Eliza Sherwood, (9/ 11/ 1797),*
>
> *Louisa Sherwood, (26/ 02/ 1804),* 15/02/2011.
>
> *Violet Sherwood, (23/ 02/ 1803),*

Online Gallery:

http://www.bl.uk/onlinegallery/onlineex/apac/photocoll/ m/019pho0000247s2u00034000.html,

Military Orphan School, Calcutta, 15/02/2011.

Familysearch.org Searches

Free Family History and Geneology Records

Individual Record:

> *Ade de St. Valery, (About 1044), France,* 3/2/2012.
>
> *Mary Caroline Newmarch, Born 23/10/1842, France, 18/03/2012.*

India Marriages, 1792-1948:

> *Charles Douglas Newmarch, (21/3/1853),*
>
> *Henry Newmarch, (1/6/1820),*
>
> *Henry Fowler Newmarch, (1st Marriage), (1/01/1857), 12/02/2011.*
>
> *Henry Fowler Newmarch, (2nd Marriage), (14/01/1864),* 6/02/2011.
>
> *Isobel Newmarch, (15/10/1888),*
>
> *John Newmarch, (8/02/1854),* 6/02/2011.
>
> *Oliver Richardson Newmarch, (20/03/1858),* 3/02/2012.
>
> *Violet Sherwood, (1/6/1820),* 5/02/2011).

India Births and Baptisms, 1786-1947:

> *Alfred Newmarch, (5/05/1867),* 14/02/2011.
>
> *Alice Maude Newmarch, (31/12/1864),*
>
> *Amy Newmarch, (2/10/1861),*
>
> *Charles Newmarch, (4/12/1864),* 9/02/2011.
>
> *Charles Henry Newmarch, (1/04/1858),*
>
> *Ethel Amy Newmarch, (2/10/1861),*
>
> *George Newmarch, (23/5/1833),* 9/02/2011.
>
> *Henry Fowler Newmarch, 13/09/1831,* 5/02/2011.

Honor Newmarch, 15/05/1861),

Isobel Newmarch, (1/07/1863), 3/02/2012.

James Parke Newmarch, (28/01/1867),

John Newmarch, 10/05/1860, 11/02/2011.

Leofrie Adan Newmarch, (5/10/1863), 12/02/2011.

Lucy Curr Newmarch, (15/02/1867),

Minnie Newmarch, (4/12/1872), 11/02/2011.

Oliver Henry Norman Newmarch, ((10/11/1876),

Robert Newmarch, 19/08/1862, 9/02/2011.

Thomas Haggerston Newmarch, (11/07/1859),

Violet Newmarch, ((23/02/1824), 3/02/2012.

Violet Anna Newmarch, (16/11/1859),

Walter Newmarch, (13/02/1865), 10/02/2011

India Deaths and Burials, 1719-1948. 9/02.2011.

Elizabeth Newmarch, (7/10/1862), 12/02/2011.

International Geneological Index Records British Isles

John Newmarch, Born 14/8/1822),

Died 23/8/1822), 30/01/2012.

Robert Newmarch, 30/01/2012.

Thomas Newmarch, 20/01/2012.

William Newmarch, 14/09/2012.

International Geneological Index Records: Southwest Pacific.

Alfred Newmarch,

Alice M. Newmarch,

George Frederick Newmarch, Marriage 21/5/1874, NZ

Harriet G. Newmarch,

Henry Fowler Newmarch,

Marianne Eliza Julia Newmarch,

Violet M. Newmarch,

Walter Newmarch, Death (1925), Australia, 29/08/2011
England Marriages, 1538-1973:

George Newmarch, (17/02/1683), 27/08/2011.

Henry Newmarch, (26/06/1736), 9/02/2011.

Jeremiah Newmarch, (4/02/1724), 25/08/2011.

John Newmarch, (27/05/1638), 25/08/2011.

John Newmarch, (1641), 27/08/2011.

John Newmarch, (26/11/1685), 14/09/2011.

John Newmarch, (7/03/1696), 14/09/2011.

John Newmarch, (11/04/1700), 25/08/2011.

Joseph Newmarch, (1722), 27/08/2011.

Joseph Newmarch, (27/4/1779), 17/02/2011.

Richard Newmarch, (8/05/1610), 25/08/2011.

Richard Newmarch, (20/09/1618), 24/08/2011.

Robert Newmarch, (30/10/1574), 24/08/2011.

Robert Newmarch, (25/01/1578), 24/08/2011.

Robert Newmarch, (3/06.1588), 23/02/2011.

Robert Newmarch, (17/01/1592), 23/02/2011.

Robert Newmarch, (26/04/1601), 23/02/2011.

Robert Newmarch, (2/06/1607), 23/02/2011.

Thomas Newmarch, (25/10/1716), 20/01/2012.

William Newmarch, (11/8/1636), 25/08/2011.

William Newmarch, (20/03/1645), 25/08/2011.

William Newmarch, (2/06/1730), 25/08/2011.

William Newmarch, (24/02/1754), 25/08/2011.

William Newmarch, (13/11/1756), 25/08/2011.

William Newmarch, (27/06/1773), 25/08/2011.

James Doddington Sherwood, (30/04/1823).
16/02/2011.

England Births and Christenings, 1538-1975

Agnnes Newmarch, (2/01/1564), 24/08/2011.

Agnes Newmarch, (14/04/1619), 25/08/2011.

Ann Newmarch, (6/09/1643), 27/08/2011.

Anne Newmarch, (4/6/1700), 14/09/2011.

Anne Newmarch, (7/11/1699), 14/09/2011.

Benjamin Newmarch, (12/02/1700), 14/09/2011.

Bernard Newmarch, ((7/11/1858), 28/08/2011.

Charles Henry Newmarch, (6/08/1824), 6/02/2011.

Douglas Newmarch, 1880, 11/02/2011.

Elizabeth Newmarch, (29/04/1623), 25/08/2011.

(Female) Newmarch, (8/07/1675), 24/08/2011.

(Female) Newmarch, (1698), 24/08/2011.

Francis Newmarch, (27/10/1580), 25/08/2011.

Frank Newmarch, 1879, 11/02/2011.

George Frederick Newmarch, (19/09/1817), 6/02/2011.

George Newmarch, (25/12/1644), 27/08/2011.

Georgius Newmarch, (14/04/1672), 27/08/2011.

George Newmarch, (7/01/1791), 17/02/2011.

Henry Newmarch, (23/02/1798), 5/02/2011.

Hester Newmarch, 1877, 11/02/2011.

Honor Ward, (22/11/1757), 25/08/2011.

Jane Newmarch, (25/01/1589), 25/08/2011.

Jane Newmarch, (09/02/1610), 25/08/2011.

Jeremiah Newmarch, (31/08/1762), 24/08/2011.

Jeremiah Newmarch, (22/02/1729), 18/02/2011.

John Newmarch, (26/12/1607), 15/09/2011.

John Newmarch, (27/12/1612), 24/08/2011.

John Newmarch, (27/05/1638), 25/08/2011.

John Newmarch, (14/08/1648), 27/08/2011.

John Newmarch, (4/03/1685), 24/08/2011.

John Newmarch, (14/08/1822), 21/02/2011.

Joseph Newmarch, (1/9/1646), 25/08/2011.

Joseph Newmarch, (11/12/1697), 27/08/2011.

Joseph Newmarch, (13/08/1732), 11/09/2011.

Joseph Newmarch, (10/08/1747), 25/08/2011.

Joseph Newmarch, (About 1754), 17/02/2011.

Joseph Newmarch, (26/06/1795), 7/02/2011.

(Male) Newmarch, (1696), 20/01/2012.

(Male) Newmarch, (6/02/1742), 24/08/2011.

Marian Newmarch, (9/02/1802), 17/02/2011.

Marie Newmarch, (09/1647), 25/08/2011.

Oliver Newmarch, 1876, 11/021675)/2011.

Richard Newmarch, (8/05/1610), 24/08/2011.

Robert Newmarch, (31/07/1587), 23/02/2011.

Robtus Newmarsh, (20/08/1596), 23/02/2011.

Robert Newmarch, (27/4/1651), 25/08/2011.

Sarah Newmarch, (8/04/1792), 17/02/2011.

Thomas Newmarch, (5/01/1715), 26/08/2011.

Thomas Newmarch, (6/04/1735), 24/08/2011.

Thomas Newmarch, (25/02/1732), 25/08/2011.

William Newmarch, (15/09/1575), 25/08/2011.

William Newmarch, (5/03/1583), 30/01/2012.

William Newmarch, (7/02/1601), 30/01/2012.

Willm Newmarche, (23/05/1621), 30/01/2012.

William Newmarch, (20/03/1645), 25/08/2012.

William Newmarch, (11/08/1636), 25/08/2011.

William Newmarch, (15/9/1717), 20/01/2012.

William Newmarch, (14/04/1726), 25/08/2011.

William Newmarch, (2/02/1733), 26/08/2011.

William Cock Newmarch, (28/10/1738), 25/08/2011.

William Newmarsh, (17/6/1739), 22/01/2012.

William Newmarch, (29/10/1747), 22/01/2012.

William Newmarch, (26/03/1757), 14/11/2011.

Diana Ward, (21/3/1790), 25/08/2011.

Thomas Watson, (1693), 12/02/2012.

England Deaths and Burials, 1538-1991:

Alice Newmarch, (2/08/1656), 27/08/2011.

Agnes Newmarch, (12/09/1595), 25/08/2011.

Agnes Newmarch, (21/03/1620), 25/08/2011.

Anna Newmarch, (21/10/1679), 27/08/2011.

Francis Newmarch, (24/06/1586), 25/08/2011.

George Newmarch, (27/08/2011), 27/08/2011.

Joseph Thompson Newmarch, (8/04/1809), 7/02/2011.

(Male) Newmarch, (24/4/1685), 25/08/2011.

Martha Newmarch, (26/03,1705), 27/08/2011.

Richard Newmarch, (2/02/1590), 25/08/2011.

Richardus Nowmarch, (24/04/1631), 25/08/2011.

Robert Newmarch, (15/12/1590), 24/08/2011.

William Newmarch, (18/03/1647), 25/08/2011.

Major General James Doddington Sherwood, (26/01/1837).

England & Wales Census, 1891:

George Fred. Newmarch, age 73 years, Burford, 6/02/2011.

http://en.wikipedia.org/wiki/Barbican

Barbican, 6/03/2012.

http://en.wikipedia.org/wiki/Battle_Abbey_Roll,
> *Battle Abbey Roll*, 7/09/2011.

http://en.wikipedia.org/wiki/Battle,_East_Sussex,
> *Battle, East Sussex*, 10/05/2012.

http://en.wikipedia.org/wiki/Bayeux_Tapestry
> *Bayeux Tapestry*, 5/06/2012.

http://en.wikipedia.org/wiki/Bernard_de_Neufmarche,
> *Bernard de Neufmarche*, 6/3/2012.

http://en.wikipedia.org/wiki/Bill_of_attainder,
> *Bill of Attainder*, 13/02/2012.

http://en.wikipedia.org/wiki/
Church_of_St._John_of_Beverley,_Whatton,
> *Church of St.John of Beverley, Whatton*, 7/09/2011.

http://en.wikipedia.org/wiki/
Companions_of_William_the_Conqueror,
> *Companions of William the Conqueror*, 7/09/2011.

http://en.wikipedia.org/wiki/Company_Rule_in_India ,
> *Company Rule in India*, 17/3/2012.

http://en.wikipedia.org/wiki/Demense,
> *Demense, 1/03/2012.*

http://en.wikipedia.org/wiki/Dover_Castle,
> *Dover Castle, 22/05/2012.*

http://en.wikipedia.org/wiki/Escheat,
> *Escheat, 1/03/2012.*

http://en.wikipedia.org/wiki/Knight's_fee,
> *Knight's Fee*, 31/01/2012.

http://en.wikipedia.org/wiki/Marquess_of_Rockingham,
> *Marquess of Rockingham*, 11/02/2012.

http://en.wikipedia.org/wiki/Martello_tower,

Martello Tower, 17/5/2012.

http://en.wikipedia.org/wiki/

Thomas_Watson_Wentworth,_1st_Marquess__of_Rockingham

Thomas Watson-Wentworth, 1st Marquess of Rockingham, 12/02/2012.

http://en.wikipedia.org/wiki/Walmer_Castle

Walmer Castle, 19/05/2012.

http://en.wikipedia.org/wiki/Wardships,_etc._Act_1267,

Wardships,etc. Act 1267, 1/03/2012.

http://en.wikipedia.org/wiki/Warren_(free),

Warren (free), 2/04/2012.

http://en.wikipedia.org/wiki/Wentworth_Castle,

Wentworth Castle, 6/02/2012.

http://en.wikipedia.org/wiki/Wentworth_Woodhouse,

Wentworth Woodhouse, 8/02/2012.

http://en.wikipedia.org/wiki/Whig_(British_political_Party),

Whig (British Political Party), 12/02/2012.

http://en.wikipedia.org/wiki/

Yeoman#14th_to_18th_centuries,

Yeoman, 17/03/2012.

http://en.wikipedia.org/wiki/York_city_walls,

York City Walls, 6/03/2012.

http://en.wikisource.org/wiki/Bernard_(fl.1093)_(DNBOO),

Bernard (fl.1093) (DNBOO), 16/05/2012.

http://familysearch.org/pal:MM9.1.1/XQHJ-WDG,

England and Wales Census: for Henry F Newmarch, 22/03/2012.

http://geograph.org.uk/article/Wealden-Hall-Houses,

Wealden Hall Houses, 17/05/2012.

http://history.ac.uk/cmh/gaz/personsN.html#N,

    Gazetteer of Markets and Fairs to 1516: Index of Persons
    28/01/2012.

http://www.houseofnames.com/newmarch-coat-of-arms,

    Newmarch Coat of Arms and Name History, 7/09/2011.

http://search.Ancestry.com.au/content/viewerpf.aspx?
h=8361563&db=uki1881&iid=KENRG11_960_965-0089&sp=
0, 1881 Census record for Alfred Newmarch, 5/02/2011.

http://trove.nla.gov.au/ndp/del/printArticlePdf/
17688497/3?print=n

    Sydney Morning Herald Article 12th June, 1940:
    Mr. Alfred Newmarch, 22/12/2012.

http://www.medievalgeneology.org.uk/guide/vis.shtml,

    Heralds Visitations and the College of Arms, 6/02/2012.

http://www.bl.uk/onlinegallery/onlineex/apac/photocoll/
m/019pho0000247s2u00034000.html,

    Military Orphan School Calcutta, 15/02/2011.

http://www.castles99.ukprint.com/Essays/glasbury.html,

    Glasbury Castle, 04/10/2011.

http://wiki.familysearch.org/en/India_Military_Records,

    India Military Records, 14/02/2011.

http://wiki.fibis.org/index.php?
title=Orphans#Upper_Orphan_School,

    Orphans, 15/02/2011.

http://www.history.ac.uk/cmh/gaz/gazweb2.html,

    Gazetteer of Markets and Fairs in England and Wales to
    1516: Nottinghamshire, 28/01/2012.

http://www.nationalarchives.gov.uk/documents/research-
guides/markets-and-fairs.htm,

Early Markets and Fairs, 28/01/2012.

Parry, Edward, *Brecon Castle: In the town of Brecon, Powys, Mid Wales S O 044 286.*

http://WWW.BRECONCASTLE.CO.UK, 1988.

http://yourarchives.nationalarchives.gov.uk/index.php?title=Napoleon_on_St_Helena#Flagships_stationed_at_the_Island, *Napoleon on St. Helena,* 17/03/2012.

http://www.rmg.co.uk/explore/sea-and-ships/in-depth/nelson-and-napoleon/english/aftermath/exile-on-st-helena, *Exile on St. Helena,* 17/03/2012.

http://www.visionofbritain.org.yk/place/place_page.jsp?p_id=11517, *History of Barnby upon Don, in Doncaster and Yorkshire/ Map and Description,* 3/03/2012.

www.britishancestors.com

Research Joseph Newmarch, 18/01/2012.

York Archives:

York Herald Advertisement: *27/10/1792, 19/10/1799, "Joseph Newmarch, at his tea, sugar and spice warehouse,*

York Herald, *"York, To be let," 14/3/1795, 3/3/1798.*

York Gazette, *"Yesterday in the 58th year of her age, Mrs. Newmarch...."* (Death Notice for Honor Newmarch), *(23/12/1816).*

York Gazette, " at Altrincham, in the 77th year of his age", *18/10/ 1823,* (Joseph Newmarch Death Notice),

York Gazette, *"Newmarch - On the 22nd instant, at 74 Micklegate, in this city, aged 68 years, Henry Newmarch, Esq., M.D., late surgeon of the Bengal Army", 30/06/1866.*

The Genealogical Table

Agnes= BERNARD DE NEWMARCH= Nesta

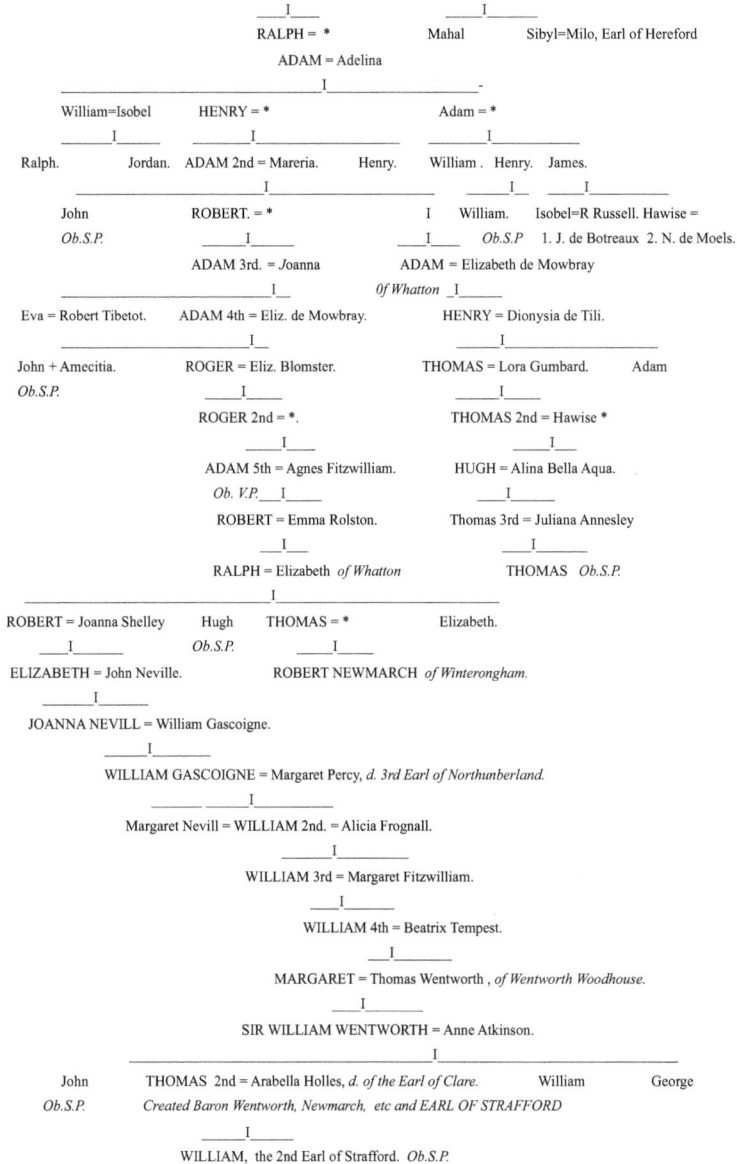

```
        ___I___                    ___I___
        RALPH = *              Mahal        Sibyl=Milo, Earl of Hereford
        ADAM = Adelina
```

```
_____I_____-
William=Isobel    HENRY = *                    Adam = *
      _____I_____      _____I_____      _____I_____
Ralph.        Jordan.  ADAM 2nd = Mareria.  Henry.   William . Henry.  James.
_____I_____   _____I__  ___I_____
        John          ROBERT. = *              I    William.   Isobel=R Russell. Hawise =
        Ob.S.P.           _____I_____       ___I____  Ob.S.P   1. J. de Botreaux  2. N. de Moels.
                      ADAM 3rd. = Joanna      ADAM = Elizabeth de Mowbray
_____I__      Of Whatton _I_____
Eva = Robert Tibetot.  ADAM 4th = Eliz. de Mowbray.    HENRY = Dionysia de Tili.
_____I__                 _____I_____
John + Amecitia.    ROGER = Eliz. Blomster.     THOMAS = Lora Gumbard.      Adam
Ob.S.P.                 _____I_____                 _____I____
                    ROGER 2nd = *.              THOMAS 2nd = Hawise *
                        ___I____                     ___I____
                    ADAM 5th = Agnes Fitzwilliam.   HUGH = Alina Bella Aqua.
                    Ob. V.P.__I____                 ___I_____
                    ROBERT = Emma Rolston.      Thomas 3rd = Juliana Annesley
                        ___I__                       ___I_____
                    RALPH = Elizabeth of Whatton    THOMAS  Ob.S.P.
_____I_____
ROBERT = Joanna Shelley   Hugh     THOMAS = *          Elizabeth.
    ___I_____          Ob.S.P.        ___I____
ELIZABETH = John Neville.          ROBERT NEWMARCH of Winterongham.
    _____I_____
JOANNA NEVILL = William Gascoigne.
        _____I_____
WILLIAM GASCOIGNE = Margaret Percy, d. 3rd Earl of Northunberland.
        _____ ___I_____
Margaret Nevill = WILLIAM 2nd. = Alicia Frognall.
                _____I_____
            WILLIAM 3rd = Margaret Fitzwilliam.
                ___I_____
            WILLIAM 4th = Beatrix Tempest.
                __I_____
            MARGARET = Thomas Wentworth , of Wentworth Woodhouse.
                ___I_____
            SIR WILLIAM WENTWORTH = Anne Atkinson.
_____I_____
John      THOMAS 2nd = Arabella Holles, d. of the Earl of Clare.   William   George
Ob.S.P.   Created Baron Wentworth, Newmarch, etc and EARL OF STRAFFORD
                _____I_____
            WILLIAM, the 2nd Earl of Strafford. Ob.S.P.
```

This section of the Genealogical Table, is as recorded in The Newmarch Pedigree.

249

The Genealogical Table Part II

This section continues from Robert Newmarch of Winteringham in Part 1. Although the author cannot be certain that this is the correct link, (as there are many possibilities), the literature supports the data given below as a plausible link in respect to: continuation of family names, reasonably localized area in North Lincolnshire, and credible dates. The difficulty comes as there are a number of Newmarch families in the same area between 1550 and 1600, who are possible links. However, I offer the following:

ROBERT NEWMARCH = Catherine Dyson 25/1/1578 Barton-upon-Humber

Robert 31/7/1587-15/9/1590 ROBERT 20/8/1596 = Elizabeth
(Barton-upon-Humber) (Barrow-upon-Humber)

ROBERT = Elizabeth

ROBERT MARCH (Born ABOUT 1621) = Margaret Hanson (M. 21/5/1644, Great Limber)

Robert March (12/3/1644 Great Limber)

JOHN MARCH (24/12/1646) = Mary Tomson (M. 11/7/1670, Cabourne)

John March (1672) EDWARD MARCH (01/1674, Cabourne) = Alicia (Abt.1700, Rothwell)

Sarah (1704) WILLIAM (6/1/1710, Rothwell) = Elizabeth (1739 Rothwell)
(Died Wrawby 06/1756)

Elizabeth (1711) JOSEPH (10/8/1747, Wrawby) = Honor Ward (26/4/1779, York).

George	Sarah	Joseph	Harriet	HENRY	Honor	Marion
7/1/1791	8/4/1792	26/6/1795	1/11/1796	23/2/1798	23/8/1799	9/2/1802

George = Mary (Continues Part III, Next Page).

George Frederick John Charles Henry
17/9/1817 14/8/1822 1824

(Authors of The Newmarch Pedigree).

The Genealogical Table Part III

DR. HENRY NEWMARCH = Violet Sherwood (M. 1/6/1820).

(B. 23/2/1798, York)   (B. 1803, Bengal India)

Surgeon 2nd Brigade Horse Artillery, India

CHILDREN

1. Violet , Christened, 23/2/ 1824, Calcutta, W. Bengal, India

2. Charles Douglas, Born 1828, India = Annie Weaver Windyer (21/3/1853, Calcutta Bengal India). - 1. Charles Henry B. 1/4/1858, D. 1/4/1858)

3. HENRY FOWLER   Born 7/2/1832, Kumaul, Wesr Bengal, India ---See Part IV.

4. George, Born 23/5/1833, Cawnpore Bengal, India. (Lt. Col. Royal Engineers).

   Married Emily Elizabeth Tribe, 1854, Chatham, Kent, England.

   1. Stanley Charles 4/12/1858 - 21/5/1860, Bengal, India.

   2. Amy 29/11/1861, Lahore, West Bengal, India.

   3. Isobel 23/8/1863, Simla, Calcutta, West Bengal, India.
   M. Alexander H. Gordon (15/10/1888), Murree, W. Bengal, India

   4. Ethel Annie, 7/1/1865, Lahore W. Bengal, India.

5. Oliver Richardson, B. 1835. Bengal, India - Major-General Sir Oliver
   Richardson Newmarch - Military Secretary to the India Office 1889-1899.
   Knight Commander of the Order of the Star of India.

   M. 1. Mary Isabella Parke, 1831 - 1871. Married 20/3/1858, Mussourie, W. Bengal

   1. Violet Anna, 16/11/1859, Mussourie, M. Wilfnorman M. 1/9/1885, Simla.

   2. Honor, 26/6/1861, Futtehgul, West Bengal.

   3. Alice Maude, 31/12/1864, Allahabad. M. Arthur Barclay, 14/3/1885, India.

   4. Janie Parke, 10/2/1867, W. Bengal India. M. Alexander Bulstrode Fenton, 1884, Simla, India.

   M. 2. Agnes Mary Norman, M. 3/3/1874, Calcutta, West Bengal, India.

   1. Oliver Henry Norman 10/11/1876, Simla, West Bengal, India.

* Abbreviations

Ob.S.P.	Obiit sine prole. (Died without issue)
Ob.V.P.	Died without living children
M	Married
D	Died

251

The Genealogical Table IV

COLONEL HENRY FOWLER NEWMARCH, Bengal Staff Corps, India.

Born 7/2/1832, Kumaul, West Bengal, India.

M. 1. 1/1/1857, Elizabeth Barnes Sparks, Daughter of Mitchell George Sparks.

    1. Henry , 17/8/1858, Peshawar, Bengal India.

        M. Kate Adelaide, D. 4/10/1942, British Columbia.

    2. John, 10/5/1860, Saugor, India.

    3. Robert, 19/8/1862, Saugor, Bengal, India.

M. 2. 14/1/1864, Marianne Eliza Juliana, Daughter of Alfred Davies., Calcutta,

    Bengal, India.

    1. Walter, 13/2/1865, Bhandara, Bengal, India.

  * 2. ALFRED, 29/8/1865, Bhandara, West Bengal, India.

    3. Charles, 13/4/1869, ? London, ? Allahabad, India.

    4. George, 1870, London, England.

    5. Minnie, 4/12/1872, Seetabuldee, West Bengal, India.

    6. Oliver, 1876, London, England.

    7. Hester, 1877, Herne Bay, Kent, England.

    8. Frank, 1879, London, England.

    9. Douglas, 1880, Sturry, Kent, England

ALFRED = Harriet Mary Robinson M. 1889 Ashfield, Sydney Australia
_____I_____

Alice Mary B 1892	Violet M., B 1894	Harriet Catherine Gwenyth B. 1898
M Arthur Frederick Davis	M. Ashton H Gregg	M. Richmond Hull Chapman, Manly, 1918.
Manly 1945	Manly, 1922.	I
	I Gwen	I

_____I_____

Lois Patricia Abt. 1919	Joy Alice (18/10/21)	COLIN ALFRED B. 28/6/1926,
Manly	M. Robert Hughes	M. Betty Vivienne Hall B. 28/7/1928
I		At St. Matthew's Manly, 17/1/1948.
M. Trevor Drayton Newnham		I
Manly, 1941.		1. Wendy Lorraine, B 19/02/1950 (the Author)
I		2. Gary Colin, B 22/11/1951
1. Vivienne Gwenyth		
2. Yvonne Anne		
3. Julianne Patricia		
4. Suzanne Joy		

List of Illustrations

List of Illustrations

(Continued)

List of Illustrations

(Continued)

List of Illustrations

(Continued)

Page No.

List of Illustrations
(Continued)

* P&W = Pen and Watercolour Illustration

Areas Visited in England, Wales and France

www.ingramcontent.com/pod-product-compliance
Lightning Source LLC
Chambersburg PA
CBHW040124270326
41926CB00001B/4